THE
MILLIONAIRE MAKER'S GUIDE
TO
WEALTH CYCLE INVESTING

THE
MILLIONAIRE MAKER'S GUIDE
TO
WEALTH CYCLE INVESTING

Build Your Assets into a Lifetime of Financial Freedom

Loral Langemeier

McGraw-Hill
New York   Chicago   San Francisco
Lisbon   London   Madrid   Mexico City   Milan
New Delhi   San Juan   Seoul   Singapore
Sydney   Toronto

The McGraw-Hill Companies

1 2 3 4 5 6 7 8 9 0   DOC/DOC   0 9 8 7 6

ISBN-13: 978-0-07-147872-4
ISBN-10: 0-07-147872-8

This publication is designed to provide accurate and authoritative information in regard to the subject matter covered. It is sold with the understanding that neither the author nor the publisher is engaged in rendering legal, accounting, or other professional service. If legal advice or other expert assistance is required, the services of a competent professional person should be sought.

—From a Declaration of Principles jointly adopted
by a Committee of the American Bar
Association and a Committee of Publishers

McGraw-Hill books are available at special quantity discounts to use as premiums and sales promotions, or for use in corporate training programs. For more information, please write to the Director of Special Sales, Professional Publishing, McGraw-Hill, Two Penn Plaza, New York, NY 10121-2298. Or contact your local bookstore.

Library of Congress Cataloging-in-Publication Data

Langemeier, Loral.
   The millionaire maker's guide to wealth cycle investing / by Loral Langemeier.
      p. cm.
   ISBN 0-07-147872-8 (alk. paper)
   1. Finance, Personal.   2. Investments.   3. Wealth.   I. Title.
HG179.L2642   2007
332.6—dc22   2006021416

Printed on acid-free paper.

The best direct investment that I ever made was in my wonderful family. This book is for Carl, Logan, and our new arrival. Thank you for everything.

Contents

ACKNOWLEDGMENTS
ix

INTRODUCTION
1

1
All About Assets
7

2
THE WEALTH CYCLE: How Assets Drive Wealth Building
19

3
ASSETS IN THE GAP ANALYSIS: Getting from Here to There
31

4
MONEY RULES: Taking Control
57

5
GET A TEAM: Leading Your Wealth
69

6
DUE DILIGENCE: Responsibility and Risk
77

7

VALUATION: Show Me the Money

103

8

RISK: Win More, Lose Less

129

9

REAL ESTATE: Location, Land, and Leverage

139

10

PRIVATE EQUITY VENTURES: Making Business Something Personal

157

11

ENERGY: Getting Down and Dirty with Oil and Gas

169

12

ALTERNATIVE ASSETS AND MORE: Passion, Purpose, and Profits

179

13

PUTTING IT TOGETHER: Compounding Power

193

14

THE NEXT GENERATION: Building Baby Millionaires

205

FINAL WORDS

209

INDEX

211

Acknowledgments

Just as there is no such thing as a self-made millionaire, no author can go it alone. Writing a book takes a team, and, once again, I was very fortunate to have an abundance of team in this endeavor.

Thank you to everyone at McGraw-Hill, including Jeanne Glasser, Lynda Luppino, Philip Ruppel, Keith Fox, Lydia Rinaldi, and more. Thank you also to Caroline Sherman for her fabulous work. Thank you Melanie, Stacey, Wendy, and the Premier team for helping get the word out for our joint venture.

Thank you to those who were willing to lend their time and attention to give notes and help make this a better book. Specifically, I appreciate all the highlighting and scratch marks from Wendy Byford, Gary Bauer, Joni Moss, Jim Kaspari, Mark Meyerdirk, Kent Mitchell, Paul Miltonberger, David Mleczko, Warren Taryle, and Pam Valvano.

The content of this book was greatly aided by comments from my field partners, Fred Auzenne, Robert Couch, Bill Curosh, Carl Logrecco, Steve Parker, Jay Pearson, James Shephard, Ken Starks, Sue Walker, and David Zebny. They are out there creating the ventures that are so rewarding to so many, and I'm glad to be a part of their pursuits.

Thank you to the home team at Live Out Loud. I can always count on the resourcefulness and initiative of our great strategists, coaches, field partners, and those on the front lines digging through the details. Special thanks to Tina Roig and Rebekah Hall for helping to coordinate my life with my business and making sure that things happen when they should.

Thank you to everyone in the Live Out Loud community and those who participate in the Big Tables and Coaching Programs. Wealth Cycles are only as good as the people who make them, and these people keep it all so good. Continue to create!

My mom and dad and siblings, Jeff, Doug, Kent, and Holly, were the first to teach me about team, and I still benefit from their support and encouragement; thank you. I'm also very grateful to my Aunt Bev, who helped me make that first and pivotal investment in myself.

Most of all, thank you to Carl, my son Logan, and our newest team member for the great life we have together.

THE
MILLIONAIRE MAKER'S GUIDE
TO
WEALTH CYCLE INVESTING

INTRODUCTION

The time has come for a new approach to investing. If you're willing to take action right now and take control of your finances, then you and I are having the same conversation. I can help you become a millionaire in three to five years.

This approach is not only exciting and rewarding but also empowering. Once you get into Wealth Cycle Investing, you will be more in control of your financial future than you ever thought possible. Not only will you become wealthy, but your days will be more interesting and dynamic than you could ever have imagined. Best of all, through wealth building, you will improve every aspect of your life. And anyone can do it.

Potential investors come in four types.

TYPE 1 has nothing. This investor rents a house or an apartment, has a decent job that pays enough to break even after taxes, and has a little money in the bank, but has even more in debt, most likely on credit cards. This type is often caught in an endless cycle of making money and spending money.

TYPE 2 has slightly more than nothing. This investor is similar to Type 1 but has also managed to put some money into an IRA and maybe some mutual funds.

TYPE 3 has bought a house or an apartment and has some investments in the form of an IRA, stock market funds, or maybe a 401(k). I find that most people who identify themselves as middle-class folk are of this type.

TYPE 4 is the cash-poor millionaire. This type has a million dollars or more tied up in underperforming—that is, lazy—assets. These assets usually consist of a primary home that's appreciated over the years, maybe a vacation house, 401(k)s, IRAs, and a fund or two. Despite their impressive net worth, cash-poor millionaires live month to month in the same endless cycle of make-spend, make-spend as the other types.

Become a millionaire in three to five years; Wealth Cycle Investing puts you in control of your financial future.

Perhaps you can identify with one of these types, or perhaps you are somewhere in between. Regardless of the type, too many people seem to be working very hard to build a financial life that ends up being a whole lotta nothing. And that's not okay. They need to be a part of Wealth Cycle Investing. The complete Wealth Cycle, which was fully explained in my last book, *The Millionaire Maker,* is a process in which income and assets are continuously created. The investing piece, which is the subject of this book, gets you to a place where you are making more money available for investing, learning about different investment opportunities, gathering a team to help you invest, and investing directly in the kinds of assets that will make you a millionaire. Millionaire-making assets are those that

- Provide investors with higher-than-market returns
- Allow investors to hedge risk
- Optimize investors' energy, efforts, and money

Traditional investing alone may or may not make you wealthy. I don't know about you, but if I'm going to make the effort to invest, I want to get wealthy doing it.

The problem is that when most people think of investing, they think of owning pensions, IRAs, mutual funds, and a primary home. Some think stocks, maybe bonds, insurance vehicles, annuities, and possibly a second home. These are investments, it's true, but unless you're very lucky, these are not the investments that will make you a millionaire in a timely or sustainable way.

Traditional investing alone may or may not make you wealthy.

If you want to be a millionaire—a real millionaire, not just a millionaire on paper—you need to go beyond traditional investment vehicles such as pensions, IRAs, mutual funds, home ownership, and stocks. Building a million-dollar portfolio requires the type of assets and strategies that the wealthy have always used to

- Generate cash
- Grow their net worth

These assets include income-generating and appreciating real estate properties, private business ventures, and other such investments. Wealth Cycle Investing strategies include making more money, building more assets, structuring entities to benefit from tax laws, and leveraging OPM, or "other people's money." Many call this high-risk, high-reward investing, but I believe risk is only your failure to educate yourself about an opportunity.

Much of the risk in high-reward ventures can be reduced if you collect enough information and put together a wealth team. The wealthy did not get that way by maxing out their 401(k)s. People whom I've helped educate have portfolios that include dozens of cash-flow-generating houses, exciting new start-up companies, and even oil wells. That's right, oil wells. Not the stocks that represent the oil companies, but the honest to goodness dirty drilling rigs.

This shift in your approach to investing can put you on the road to generating and sustaining great wealth in just three to five years. That's true no matter when or where you begin this process, whether you have underperforming investments (lazy assets) or you have nothing and are in debt.

I was in the latter group when I made the decision to become a millionaire. At the time, I was sleeping on friends' couches and had no assets to speak of, let alone much cash in my pocket. I grew up on a farm in Nebraska, went to college on some scholarships and my own dime, and spent much of my life working hard for grades and money. In my teens, I created a health and fitness business and operated it through my college years and beyond. I was brought up to believe that "you work hard for your money, and then you retire." Looking back, that now reads to me as "limit your life until you die." But that's the path I was on. "Work hard for your money" was my core belief. It was based on a childhood of that type of conditioning, handed down from my parents, who got it from their parents, who got it from their parents, and so on.

After college, I landed a senior-level job at a Fortune 500 company, and fortunately, my path changed when I met people who thought very differently about earning and investing. They were making money the way the wealthy had made it for generations. Instead of working at jobs with a fixed wage and an ultimate salary cap, they were creating their own companies, pursuing entrepreneurial ventures, and using that money to invest in and develop more assets. That was the secret formula of the wealthy: managing and building a portfolio that created even greater wealth.

Eventually, I turned off that "stay small and work hard for your money" neon sign in my brain and decided to reach out for the bigger, better life I'd always dreamed of. I took charge of my wealth and made a commitment to become a millionaire. At that time I owned nothing but my car and a small savings account. I was also pregnant and preparing to be a single mother. The commitment was prompted by a colleague, who basically told me, "Single mothers can't be millionaires; it's too hard. You're doomed." Sick to my stomach with his decree, I became even more determined. And a few weeks before my thirty-fourth birthday, I became a millionaire. Even better, through investments and involvement in my business, my seven-year-old son, Logan, is well on his way to becoming a millionaire as well.

I did all of this by creating and executing the Wealth Cycle, an approach that helps you accumulate wealth *and* have ready cash to enjoy a better life. The Wealth Cycle consists of 12 building blocks geared to creating wealth. These

> *The Wealth Cycle helps you accumulate wealth and have ready cash to enjoy a better life.*

include entrepreneurship and entity structuring as well as forecasting strategies, debt management, team building, and leadership. This book focuses on the building block of direct asset allocation, or what Wall Street calls DPP, direct participation programs. In the Wealth Cycle, we simply call them *assets.*

My approach is not difficult, it's just different. All it takes is collecting knowledge and getting a team together to execute your strategy so that you are successful. Neither of these is that hard. In fact, the first step I took to accelerate my investments was a simple call. I picked up the phone and found a mentor who was investing in the type of assets I wanted in my own portfolio. He helped me research that asset class, find the right deal, and put the team together to get the deal done. That is the approach that made me a multimillionaire fast, and it's how I continue to accelerate my wealth. I amass knowledge, and I get a team.

This book explains how you can build your assets by dramatically increasing your access to cash, credit, and deal flow. You learn how to invest in diverse areas, ranging from traditional equity and debt instruments such as stocks and bonds to more unconventional money-generating vehicles, including private equity, oil and gas, and a variety of real estate ventures, such as land, multitenant buildings, and commercial properties. The objective of Wealth Cycle Investing is to create above-market returns at below-market risk. Any investor can do this—and that means you. Whether you are a Type 1, who needs to make something out of nothing, a Type 4, with lazy assets that need waking up, or somewhere in between, you can supercharge your portfolio and create cash-flowing wealth.

> **Wealth Cycle Investing creates above-market returns at below-market risk.**

This book does not offer investment advice. Its goal is to educate you on how to create and build assets. Now you can do what all the other millionaire makers have done—invest directly in specific cash-generating and appreciating assets. Welcome to Wealth Cycle Investing.

1

All about Assets

Jed Stone was a classic Type 1. Young and single, he had a decent job, rented a small apartment in a big city, and had accumulated significant credit card debt. In the first four months of his Wealth Cycle, we helped Jed to create an additional $1,000 a month of income, structure his tax strategies to retain it, build funds for investing, manage his debt, and start creating assets. The first investment he made was in real estate. He bought a small house that put cash in his pocket every month. Soon, Jed was leveraging his money with other people's money in order to begin investing in more properties and other assets.

Allison Connor was in a similar boat. A Type 2, she had some money in her IRA and a mutual fund that she'd created right out of college. After meeting a mentor who bought and sold small businesses, Allison became interested in private ventures. Later she bought a Laundromat and invested in other businesses.

With a primary home under his belt, Mick Buchanan thought he was in good shape financially. A Type 3, he had several mutual funds, an IRA, and money in his 401(k). But his wife, Mary, couldn't understand why they weren't able to take a few vacations and ensure payment of their children's college tuitions. After working with me, Mick and Mary discovered and then invested in several assets, including private equity ventures that generated thousands of dollars of cash flow each month and increased their net worth.

And then there was the Type 4 cash-poor millionaire, Dee Newton. Dee, a single mother, had more than one million dollars in net worth—most of it as a result of the appreciation of her California home. She also had money in a stock market fund, a 401(k), and IRAs and money in the bank. Yet she never had enough cash at hand, and she had built up significant credit card debt to cover her monthly expenses—proof that today's millionaires are like yesterday's middle class. Most of these cash-poor individuals are actually shocked when they find out that they have a million dollars in net worth. Once Dee initiated her Wealth Cycle Investing program, she was able to shift her lazy assets into cash-flow-generating investments while, at the same time, building and accelerating her net worth.

These four examples represent the classic types of investors I run into. In each case, my team and I were able to educate and train these individuals so that they could make more money, build their assets, and accelerate their wealth. It took time and effort and education, yes, but most of all it took desire. I will show you how each of these investors built a Wealth Cycle and deployed a Millionaire Maker plan. You'll see how Jed bought his first house, Allison invested in a small business, Mick bought into private equity, and Dee played in the oil and gas market.

Wealth Cycle Investing involves *direct asset allocation,* also known as *direct participation programs.* Let me break this down.

1. **Direct.** There's no middleman. You seek out the type of asset you want to purchase, and you put your money directly into that asset. If it's a commercial property, you put a team together and buy that property. Instead of owning an anonymous stock in some public company, you buy a piece of a private equity venture where the managers know you and you know them. You don't put your money in some fund or stock and hope for the best—what I call the "park and pray" model, where you park your money in an investment and pray that someone manages it well enough to earn a profit.

2. **Asset.** I recommend investing in hard, real assets that you can see and touch, such as properties, business ventures, and even private debt instruments. There is no limit to the range and spectrum of what qualifies as a high-reward asset. It takes creativity, resourcefulness, and initiative to find or develop these assets. With an experienced team and knowledge of the asset, you can minimize the risk associated with these high rewards.

   > *In Wealth Cycle Investing, you put your money directly into an asset, with no middleman.*

3. **Allocation.** Diversification is an age-old investment strategy that works very well. It's important to include diversification in any approach to wealth building. In Wealth Cycle Investing, you allocate your assets across many different classes and types with various growths, yields, locations, teams, and time frames.

Direct asset allocation begins with a plan. To create and execute this plan, you must

- Know your investment criteria; these are your Money Rules
- Get your cash ready for investment by
    - Converting lazy assets into cash
    - Making more money
- Scout out opportunities
- Collect knowledge
- Put a team together, because
    - Someone has done what you want to do
    - You don't have to reinvent the wheel
    - Other people's experience lowers your risk
    - More help means more speed by flattening the learning curve
- Pursue field partners, experienced professionals who
    - Act as point people
    - Provide access to the direct asset investments
    - Help manage the asset
- Conduct due diligence
- Make decisions and take action

Investing to create real wealth requires action and the pursuit of higher-than-market returns. Risk is continuously minimized through *knowledge* and a *team*. By consistently managing risk through knowledge and a team, the wealth builder can venture into more rewarding deals and investments. Historically, high-reward deals were reserved for the wealthy, but Wealth Cycle Investing creates an opportunity for anyone to become wealthy.

Accredited or Not Accredited, That Is the Question

In the past, the best investments—those with the highest returns—were reserved for accredited investors. These are investors who already have a high income or more than a million dollars in net worth. Originally, this barrier to entry was established to protect those who had little to lose from losing it all. But to me, it seems that the practice did just the opposite; it made investing solely the playground of the rich and left those with little money with no skin in the game. People who wanted big returns had to wait until they met the minimum financial requirements established by the Securities and Exchange Commission (SEC).

While it's an interesting political comment to say that the rich get richer and the poor get poorer, the truth is, the rich and the poor aren't even having the same conversation, let alone accessing the same wealth-building and tax strategies. The investing opportunities that await those who are considered accredited investors offer much higher rewards than those that are available to everyone else. That's why when you engage in Wealth Cycle Investing it's important for you to reach accredited status as soon as possible.

The good news is that the term *accredited investor* was defined by the SEC in 1933 during the Depression, when the dollar, and certainly a million dollars, had a lot more value than it does now. In fact, according to the Consumer Price Index (CPI) conversion factor, a million dollars in 1933 was equivalent to almost $15 million in 2005.

Yet, the definition of accredited investor remains:

1. You and your spouse have $1 million net worth, *or*
2. You have an income of $200,000 yourself or $300,000 together, *or*
3. You represent a trust with $5 million in assets.

Again, that's not as daunting today as it was in 1933. There are many who would not consider themselves wealthy who have a million dollars in net worth. Of course, to many of you, these numbers are daunting. Wealth Cycle Investing helps you work your way toward them, so that you can eventually accelerate your investments and get in on the high-reward deals.

The smart financial planners, brokers, bankers, and fund managers know that this model is the way investing will be done in the future. No matter who you are, you can bring something to the table. Maybe it's money, maybe it's credit, maybe it's ideas, maybe it's experience, maybe it's people, or maybe it's your time and energy. All these things are valued by the financial community.

The importance of being an accredited investor can't be emphasized enough. If you are accredited, you are eligible to invest in more direct asset allocation opportunities. When I work with people who have little in the way of assets, income, or anything else, but who want a quick acceleration of their Wealth Cycle, I suggest that they put together a team, make more money to qualify for accreditation, and do that by first getting in on diversified high-risk, high-reward deals that don't require accreditation.

Get a Team

Smart investors build and work closely with a team, because having a team reduces risk. By gathering a team of mentors—whether industry professionals, colleagues, or friends—you can

- Efficiently collect information and knowledge
- Enjoy the advantages of other people's experiences
- Hear about new deals

- Gain access to deals
- Leverage your money or credit with other people's money or credit
- Further diversify your investments

And that's just the beginning. Seeking and finding the best professionals in your asset class, gathering like-minded peers with whom you can join forces, and hiring the support you need to make the best use of your time are all essential to building assets.

Building a team makes sense, and it's not that difficult. For example, if you're involved in a lucrative real estate deal, you'll need a good lawyer. You'll find one by calling people who have done large real estate deals and asking for recommendations. You don't have to know these people personally; you just have to have the confidence to pick up the phone and ask them the question. This is one of many action steps that wealth building requires. If you're shy and nervous about taking this step, that's okay.

> *When people tell me they don't have time, I tell them they need a team. Having a team reduces your risk and affords you extra time, added support, and more access.*

But don't let your fear stop you from moving forward. Make the call. It will be easier the second time and a walk in the park the tenth.

Make More Money

If you don't meet accredited investor status, you need to find ways to make more money. Look at your current assets, if any, and figure out how they could perform better. Then consider your skill sets and devise a business venture. In the Wealth Cycle, this is your "Cash

Machine." The Cash Machine is not a dream business, but a practical money-making operation that will start generating revenue immediately and is pursued in conjunction with your current job. For example, I suggest that teachers start a tutoring business on the side, or that a craftsperson consider selling his or her furniture on eBay. Additionally, I suggest that you structure entities, such as corporations or partnerships, around these businesses to support tax strategies that allow you to retain more of your income. By making and retaining more money, you can begin to fund your Wealth Account and accelerate your journey to becoming an accredited investor.

Start with Deals You Can Do

There are investments and deals with higher-than-market-average returns that do not have accredited investor requirements. Real estate is one area where there are opportunities for those who have not yet made their million in net worth. There are many properties that can generate real cash and provide quick growth. Real estate is a great way to work your way toward the accredited investor requirements. From there, you can get into more lucrative deals. There are also ways to get in on the deals that do have accredited investor requirements even if you're not yet accredited. The SEC allows privately placed investment opportunity to offer up to 35 nonaccredited individuals ownership in the venture. Many of these investment opportunities are put together by entrepreneurs and small businesses through private placements. While there are deal managers and entrepreneurs who won't even talk to unaccredited investors, there are many more of these small-business ventures that are legally allowed and willing to let you in on the deal. Of course, you'll need to research these small-business ventures carefully, just as you do any direct asset allocation deal, big or small, in which you can invest. Your team can help you find these.

Moving Up to a Bigger Life

Making the commitment to pursue a bigger, better life takes strength and self-confidence, absolutely. Your conditioning, those messages you've absorbed since childhood, might need to be upgraded. You *do* have wealth-building muscles; they're just atrophied, and we're going to pump them up. What you need to understand is that everything I am sharing with you in this book is doable. What you need to do is make the commitment to live out loud when it comes to money, to be open to a new way of thinking about and approaching your finances. When you live out loud, you say what you want and take action to make it happen. This is the best approach I know of for ultimately getting what you want—and it's why I named my own company Live Out Loud.

Wealth Cycle Investing takes you to your *want-to* life and away from a *have-to* life; it allows you to differentiate real risk

In Wealth Cycle Investing, you control your own life.

from perceived risk and reap the highest rewards. Somehow, we've spiraled into a permission-based society, where people sit and allow others to control their fate. They settle into a routine, do things by rote, and work hard to get an "A." In Wealth Cycle Investing, you control your own life.

The ideas that I share here are based on an educational platform that I have used to create millionaires. I want to make it very clear that these ideas do not reflect my portfolio or suggest what yours should be. When you engage and initiate the Wealth Cycle Investing approach, you are responsible for your own wealth. Investing is personal, and the choices you make must be in sync with the needs of your current situation, your financial objectives, your vision, and your values.

I know people who invest in real estate, oil and gas, and stocks. I also know people who like only Laundromats or video arcades or mobile homes, others who put their money in other people's businesses, and still others who prefer purely passive investments, such as promissory notes and private equity funds. I always recommend an asset allocation strategy that has a diverse, carefully chosen blend of assets in which you have direct control of your investment. The allocation itself is up to the individual—that's the point of being in control and leading one's wealth.

Wealth Cycle Investing takes you to a want-to life and away from a have-to life; you differentiate real risk from perceived risk and reap the highest rewards.

When you decide to initiate and develop a Wealth Cycle Investment portfolio, you absolutely must

- Do your research on each and every investment
- Continuously improve your financial awareness
- Seek expert advice on each and every investment
- Build a team to maximize capacity and minimize risk
- Never park and pray, but always control your own money
- Live a corporate life with tax advantages managed through entities
- Stay in motion, because wealth takes action
- Sequence—do the right thing at the right time, every time
- Work toward building a bigger, better life
- Live out loud to learn, teach, and help others

Assets to Assets to Assets

Good investments go beyond pensions, 401(k)s, IRAs, stocks, bonds, mutual funds, insurance vehicles, your primary home, and even your second home. Here's what I look at:

- Land and predevelopment deals
- Rental properties
- Commercial real estate
- Energy and natural resource development and production, such as oil and gas
- New product development
- Private business ventures
- Coin-operated retail businesses
- Warehouses and distribution centers
- Original equipment manufacturers
- Private money or debt, such as promissory notes

Again, I'm not looking at the stocks that represent these assets, but the businesses themselves. I encourage investors to focus on direct financial participation in the people and organizations that are creating, developing, and making the products and services that are at the heart of the capitalist system.

In his groundbreaking 1937 treatise *Think and Grow Rich* (Wilshire Book Company, 1966; rev. ed.), Napoleon Hill takes a side journey into the capitalist system and why it's important. The book summarizes Hill's secrets of success based on interviews he conducted with 500 of the world's richest men. The book has been praised for decades, and I'm one of its supporters. But I wonder if Napoleon Hill himself was aware that the book's section on capitalism is its crown jewel. In this portion, which may have been rewritten for the 1960s reprint—given Hill's tone in defending the United States of America, capitalism, and the freedom and rights we all enjoy—Hill notes that we can thank capitalism for having so much placed in our hands so easily, such as food, clothing, shelter, property and individual rights, a safe banking system, and the right to choose one's occupation and way of life.

That's all worth mentioning, absolutely, but the part I find so valuable is the credit for these rights that Hill gives to the "unseen power" and the people who "organized that power" and are "responsible for its maintenance." He goes on to say, "The name of this mysterious benefactor of mankind is capital. Capital consists not alone of money, but more particularly of highly organized, intelligent groups of men who plan ways and means of using money efficiently for the good of the public, and profitability to themselves" (p.150). This statement is almost too good to be true. In his defense of capitalism, Hill reveals the true secret of being wealthy, namely, to belong to an organized intelligent group that plans how to use money for its members' profit and for the good of all.

Now, that's what I call both interesting and helpful. If that statement doesn't make you take your money out of the hands of the banks and the brokerage houses today, I don't know what will. He's saying that there are two worlds: people who are the recipients of capital beneficence, and those who create and profit from that capital beneficence.

I'm in the latter group—and so are all the people with whom I work and those whom I help to educate on investing. Wealth Cycle investors use brains and organization to make deals, make money, and make the world a better place.

You can, and should, be part of this group, too.

The Wealth Cycle

How Assets Drive Wealth Building

Wealth Cycle Investing is a system of generating cash through a self-perpetuating cycle of assets and income. Wealth Cycle investors put money into assets that generate passive income and/or grow and appreciate. They then take the returns from these assets and use them to create, and invest in, more assets. Understanding how to initiate, grow, and sustain one's assets contributes to the success of the Wealth Cycle. Our wealth builders create a constant acceleration of assets through active, direct investment in more assets.

Wealth Cycle Investing is a system of generating cash through a self-perpetuating cycle of assets and income.

This continuous investing is the secret to creating and sustaining wealth that the wealthy have used for generations. The sequence of steps begins with getting your current situation in order, learning and researching assets, building a team, and then taking practical action to begin investing.

Steps to Build Assets

1. **Establish a Wealth Account.** A Wealth Account is an interest-bearing account into which you pay regularly from your current job, from your Cash Machine, from restructuring assets, or from other passive income. This is the pay-yourself-first concept that the wealthy have followed for years, which means that no matter what, you consistently make a monthly priority payment to your fund for investing. This happens even before you make debt payments and gives you the chance to build wealth that will pay off that debt and stop the vicious cycle of just paying debt. This is a step you can take today at any financial institution that offers interest-bearing accounts.

2. **Know your Money Rules.** In order to even begin looking at assets, you have to know which ones are right for you. These should be investments that are in line with your current situation and your future goals—your Money Rules. By looking at your current situation (your Financial Baseline) and devising your goals (your Financial Freedom Day), you can plan what you can and should do. For example, if you've established a goal of creating $3,000 of passive income a month based on $360,000 of invested assets, then you need your assets to generate an aggregate return that averages 10 percent annually. By looking at your requirements and objectives, including the need to be actively or passively involved in the asset, or to generate cash flow versus appreciation, you can focus on the optimal bucket of assets for your Wealth Cycle Investing plan. I'll discuss this step in great length in Chapter 4, "Money Rules."

3. **Research and learn about assets.** This is another step that you can take today. Begin with the *Wall Street Journal* and read about the activities and deals that are happening this week. If you're not already a reader of the *Journal*, you'll be pleasantly surprised at how easy and interesting that paper is to read. You'll get a good understanding of the vocabulary of investing and who the players are in a particular field. Then branch out to financial Web sites, where you will find overviews of the asset class you're interested in and get to know the different investing options. Publications such as *Investor's Business Daily, BusinessWeek,* and *Fortune* and research reports from Wall Street's equity analysts are also great sources of information. Though they focus on publicly traded companies, these publications provide a list of the fundamentals that analysts consider, giving you a framework to copy in your own investigations and due diligence into any asset class. These can be found on the Web through search engines. If you're interested in buying property, for instance, read the research reports on real estate investment trusts (REITs) or mortgage companies. While these won't be the assets you're going to buy, the reports will give you an understanding of the general area that you can carry over to your investments. Again, the objective here is to educate yourself about different asset types and opportunities.

4. **Find and talk to mentors who understand the assets that interest you.** If you think that the use of storage units will continue to grow in the years to come, call a local facility and speak to the owner. Introduce yourself and say that you're doing some research on the acquisition of these facilities and are looking for some guidance—if not a mentor. More than almost any

other group of people, business owners, investors, and entrepreneurs are eager to share what they know. Maybe it's because the smart ones realize that collaboration is the road to greater success and are always looking for more brains and bodies to join their team. A phone call or a letter followed by a visit to confirm the arrangement is the start of most mentor relationships. Aim high. If you have an idea for investing in real estate in a town, give the mayor's office or chamber of commerce a call and see if you can begin having one-on-one meetings with those who know where the market is headed. I've even had some clients gain access to CEOs of huge companies. Reach out and get the help and advice you need as soon as possible, well before you're ready to invest. It's all about collecting knowledge and doing the research, and these conversations can cause your learning to leapfrog. Every conversation you have now will pay off later.

5. **Find and talk to field partners who can help you access those assets.**
    Learning about assets is one thing; getting in on the deals is another. At one point, I knew I wanted to find small homes that I could purchase for little money down and that would generate monthly cash flow through rentals. I assumed that these homes would be in small, quiet, perhaps growing but not booming regions of the country— bread-and-butter America. I needed to find someone who knew where these houses were and how to get them. My assumption was that the reason such homes would be inexpensive was because they would need a little rehabilitation. As long as they had rental potential, I was willing to restore them. I started asking around, and

> *Talking about the assets that interest you will create access.*

after several conversations, I found a real estate broker in the South who knew every preforeclosure in her bustling town, and a financial planner in a Midwestern state who'd discovered a cluster of $45,000 homes that required only $6,000 in up-front costs and could easily be turned into rentals. By letting people know what I was looking for, I found field partners to work with. You'll find that if you talk about the assets that interest you, you will start to create *access*. It's very important to include your mentors in this step and get their advice. There are too many people out there who have properties, businesses, or other investments that are not good investments, and a mentor will help you separate the good from the bad. A field partner is not the person who is selling the business or deal. Instead, a field partner is usually someone with the energy and experience to be in the deal alongside you, taking the risk and putting his or her own skin in the game. If this business or deal is successful, the field partner will be in your life for a long time, so make sure it's someone you enjoy being with and whom you trust with your money and your business.

6. **Perform due diligence.** Due diligence is the most important part of the investment process. Due diligence is the process of researching and investigating the details of a deal. This begins with reading various papers and materials on the asset, continues with conversations and interviews with those involved in the asset, and, in the

> *Due diligence is the most important part of the investment process.*

case of properties and businesses, means a field visit to explore the asset. In Wealth Cycle Investing, you are responsible for everything you do, no matter how big your team is or how brilliant your mentors. This means that you must perform due diligence on each and every investment. You'll learn more about how to actually conduct due diligence in Chapter 6.

7. **Set up entities to protect the assets in which you're interested.** Once you decide to make an investment, you have to structure your financial situation to optimize your return. For example, if you're going to buy a lot of properties, you might consider establishing a limited liability company (LLC) to manage and run those companies and a trust to own the LLC. You then funnel all of the revenues and expenditures realized from those properties through that trust. In Wealth Cycle Investing, you live a corporate life, a life surrounded by and improved by legal entities in order to maintain and grow your wealth.

8. **Invest.** Once you've done your research, found your team, selected an investment, done due diligence, and set up the structures to hold your wealth, it's time to go-go-go. Making millions takes action. The Wealth Cycle requires massive action so that you gain the experience you need to unearth the evidence supporting your investment choice. That evidence will give you the confidence to go after your financial goals and reach millionaire status and beyond.

Action → Experience → Evidence → Confidence = Results

This is the step in which you take the money from your Wealth Account and invest it directly in these well-

researched cash-flow or appreciation investment opportunities.
You may also be joining forces
with others in this venture,
using other people's money or
other people's credit to better
leverage your opportunity.

*The secret of the wealthy
is that they continuously
invest and create a cycle of
turning income into assets
and assets into income.*

9. **Accelerate your returns.** When your investment generates
   money, you'll want to put a portion of that money back into
   the cycle through your Wealth Account. You can create more
   wealth only if you accelerate the wealth you have—you want
   your money in motion. The way to accelerate the Wealth
   Cycle is to continue to reinvest passive income—that is,
   profits from assets.

This is what the wealthy do. They continuously invest and create
a cycle of turning income into assets and assets into income. That's
their big secret. By modeling their approach to wealth, you too can
become wealthy.

Assessing the Assets

The wealthy pursue direct investments in a wide range of asset
classes, which include all sorts of business opportunities and investment vehicles. Once you have an asset in mind, it needs to be evaluated to determine if it is a good investment for you. The way we
assess a specific investment opportunity is by testing it with the
Wealth Cycle Investing Worksheet.

WEALTH CYCLE INVESTING WORKSHEET

ASSET UNDER CONSIDERATION:

CONTACT PERSON(S):

—SETUP—
Getting Your Money and Structures Ready

SOURCE OF FUNDS (TO BE USED TO INVEST IN THIS ASSET)

WEALTH ACCOUNT   OPM*   DEBT/BANK LOAN   RESTRUCTURING OF OTHER ASSETS

*OPM IS OTHER PEOPLE'S MONEY

ENTITIES (TO USE, OR STRUCTURE, FOR THIS DEAL)

FORECASTING (TO UTILIZE FOR THIS DEAL)

—MONEY RULES—
Making Sure the Asset Meets Your Criteria and Objectives

ROI GOAL AND PROJECTED

CASH FLOW	APPRECIATION
ACTIVE	PASSIVE

DIVERSIFICATION

Allocation   Risk/Reward   Exit Strategy

—TEAM—
Gathering Resources and Knowledge

LEADER:

FIELD PARTNER:

MENTOR(S):

PROFESSIONALS:
  Entity Specialist
  Accountant
  Bookkeeper
  Lawyer

UTILITY PLAYERS:
  Help at work
  Help at home

PARTNERS AND COLLEAGUES:

—DUE DILIGENCE—
Evaluating the Deal

DATA	DISCUSSION	DISCOVERY	DIAGNOSIS	DECISION

A separate worksheet for each of your investments will help you frame your investment decisions for direct asset allocation. Think of this as an asset evaluator. It may look complicated at first, but it is going to get very simple very quickly. Like the other resources and references used in this book, this worksheet is available at www.liveoutloud.com. It can be downloaded for your reference, and you can use it for every deal you do. Additionally, although software for modeling stock and bond portfolios has been around for years there has been little available for direct asset investors. To fill this void, we have developed the Asset Accelerator. This software enables you to input different direct-asset-investing scenarios and provides you with graphic models for your decision making. More information on this is found at www.liveoutloud.com/assets.

The following is a brief explanation of each aspect of the Wealth Cycle Investing worksheet. These will be discussed in greater detail throughout the book.

Setup: Getting Your Money and Structures Ready

Getting your money ready and creating the structures for the deal are necessary steps in initiating an investment. In Wealth Cycle Investing, you constantly manage your pipeline of available cash. It's not enough to invest and wait for the checks or, worse, let the money be reinvested for you without your say. Millionaires go make money. In order to accelerate your wealth, you need to constantly take the money you make from one investment and put it into other investments. Managing those funds and understanding how much is available and when it is available is all a part of the process. I classify money as A, B, and C money.

A money. This is cash that you have on hand in your Wealth Account; it is usually available in less than 30 days.

B money. This money takes 60 to 90 days to become available. Most likely it's in an IRA, in your home equity, or in a fund or place that will take some time and effort to turn into usable cash.

C money. C money is the least liquid of your funds. It's the money that's wrapped up in another investment, such as the property you're waiting to cash out or your 401(k) at work.

All your money must be classified so that you can put it into a plan for investing. Wealth Cycle Investing doesn't let your money sit still or allow you to forget that you have money coming in from this or that source. If you pay attention to the cash that you have coming in and classify it, you give your money the chance to always earn for you. This constant management of liquid assets can be a huge psychological shift for many investors, but it's worth the effort. As with anything else, once you get used to it, it becomes another part of the process.

In the worksheet, you'll see that when you're making an investment, you must decide where in the pipeline this money is going to come from. This is your *source of funds.* The money for a deal can come from making more money and putting it into a Wealth Account that provides funds for investments. It can also come from a true self-directed IRA account. Or perhaps it's out of the pockets of family and friends. These are A-money sources and are usually available right away.

Money can also come from working with a commercial source of funds, such as a bank, or from other investors, by leveraging one's ideas, time, energy, experience, money, or credit with other people's money or credit. This money may be available immediately, but many times it's B money. Restructuring one's assets is also a good source of B money, especially if the investor is converting lazy assets into supercharged assets.

Money will also come from the liquidation of other investments you made. This is C money, waiting to be released until the asset has gone through its life cycle. This would be considered the restructuring of an existing asset.

Setup also includes the creation of *entities* and the habit of running your revenue and expenditures through these entities. Structuring your companies and creating tax strategies in order to retain and manage your wealth are important building blocks in Wealth Cycle Investing.

Money Rules

Before you look at any investment, you must establish your own personal Money Rules. Then, as you complete each worksheet, you can determine how well the projected rewards and risks of that particular asset meet your Money Rules.

Money Rules are your financial criteria and objectives, such as

- Goals for return on investment (ROI)
- Needs for generating income in the form of cash flow, appreciation, or both
- Desire to be either an active or a passive investor or some combination of the two

Knowing your exit strategy is essential in making a good investment.

Diversification strategies are also part of Money Rules. These come from the investor's need to allocate investments into the right assets for optimal risk/return ratios. Realizing the reward from each investment, which involves an exit strategy, is essential in making a good investment. Strong diversification depends on assets that realize different rewards at different times.

Team: Building Experience

There is no such thing as a self-made millionaire. It's never happened, and it never will. All investors need a team to help them become wealthy. In Wealth Cycle Investing, you are required to get the best group together in order to reduce your risk. The first member of the team is the leader—who is always you. The rest of the team includes those listed earlier, such as a field partner, mentors, professionals, and other players. This list will help you remember to engage the team for each and every asset. For example, as you consider the deal, you need to also consider your entities, so your CPA or entity specialist must be in the loop from the get-go.

Due Diligence

Due diligence—investigating every detail of the deal—is the cornerstone of all good investing and business decisions. Investors who take the time to extensively research and investigate potential deals will make better investments. We've systemized this approach as data, discussion, discovery, diagnosis, and decision—the five Ds.

Each of the steps mentioned in this section will be covered in greater detail in the remaining chapters of the book.

3

Assets in the Gap Analysis

Getting from Here to There

The four types of investors mentioned earlier represent a wide spectrum, from those who have no assets and need to create some to those who have underperforming assets that need restructuring. Regardless of your investor type, in Wealth Cycle Investing, you will continually create new assets and restructure underperforming ones. Let's look at how the four investors I mentioned—Jed Stone, Allison Connor, Mick Buchanan, and Dee Newton—go about this process.

When I begin educating clients and they start working with my team, the first thing we do is conduct a Gap Analysis. This is a diagram that helps map the distance, the gap, between where you are and where you want to be, starting with your financial baseline and ending with your Freedom Day goal. The space between the financial baseline and Freedom Day becomes your Millionaire Maker plan. I've constructed the previously mentioned case scenarios from my experiences with several clients. The names are fictional, but the facts within the cases represent a summary of concepts and actions from real deals.

Type 1: Something from Nothing

Jed Stone was 29, single, and only mildly satisfied in his job as a manager for a chain of bike shops in and around Boston. He rented a one-bedroom apartment in Back Bay, just a few stops on the T from his office; ate out or ordered in almost every night; soaked up live music entertainment and sports events; and spent the rest of his free time at a no-frills weight-lifting gym in south Boston. Despite a decent salary, he was perpetually in debt and owned nothing. I asked him the eight questions that would help us fill in the facts in the Gap Analysis:

1. What is your monthly pretax income?
2. What are your monthly expenditures?
3. What are your assets?
4. What are your liabilities?
5. What else do you own or owe?
6. What do you want?
7. What are the skills you use to make money?
8. Are you willing to create and execute a Wealth Cycle?

Jed's answers gave us what we needed to map the gap between where he was and where he wanted to be. A strategy for investing was devised that would help him get there. Jed's annual salary was $44,000, or $3,667 a month. His monthly expenses were $2,500 and included rent, a car lease, car and renter's insurance, monthly gym fees, cable and Internet fees, and live entertainment fees. Jed had no assets. The bike retailer was small, and while it paid his health insurance, he had no 401(k), no IRA, and just about $5,000 in a bank account he had started when he was 15. Jed had a perpetual balance of $5,000 on his credit cards that he couldn't seem to shake and owed his sister $2,000 that he had borrowed the previous year to pay his taxes. His dream was to one day own a chain of weight-lifting gyms.

When I asked him how much he'd like to have invested in assets and how much cash he'd like to yield from those and other investments, Jed thought $1 million invested and $5,000 a month would be enough for him to have the kind of lifestyle he'd like. This kind of ROI (return on investment) calculation is typical. A return of $5,000 per month is $60,000 per year, which means he'd need just 6 percent interest on the million dollars he meant to invest. Well, for that he didn't need me. He could just put money in a mutual fund. We needed to work on Jed's *financial consciousness*. We talked through these numbers and ideas, and adjusted his short- and long-term goals. Given that he had no assets at all and little income, we had to create doable one-year Freedom Day goals to keep him encouraged, yet challenged.

Jed's Gap Analysis looked like this:

FREEDOM DAY GOALS

- *$1,000,000 in invested assets*
- *$10,000 a month in passive income*
- *A business of owning gyms*
- *No full-time job*

REVENUE	ASSETS	
FINANCIAL BASELINE		
PRETAX INCOME: *$3,667/MONTH*	ASSETS:	*$5,000*
EXPENDITURES: *$2,500/MONTH*	LIABILITIES:	*$7,000*
	NET WORTH:	*−$2,000*

SKILL SET: organization, communications, work-out discipline.

Jed was a clear case of perishable spending and high-lifestyle living. I was eager to help him understand that you had to *earn the lifestyle before you lived it.* To do this, we went through my entire Wealth Cycle program and discussed how important it was for Jed to make more money and pay down his debt in order to build assets. To make more money, Jed decided to help sell used gym equipment on Web auction and clearance sites. We then set him up with an LLC through which to channel the revenues and expenses of that business. Jed's one-year goal was to earn an additional $10,000 per year to reduce his debt *and* give him some money to put toward assets. Though he started making money the week he created the business, the ramp-up to consistently selling one or two items a week took some time and money. But in four months Jed was making an extra $1,000 a month.

Jed had started with nothing and had never bought or invested in an asset in his life. Although it would take some time for him to accumulate enough money in an account earmarked for investing, this extra time would give him the opportunity to collect information and develop a team while his money grew through monthly payments plus the marvel of compound interest. He would also work on his leadership skills, take control of his situation, and rethink his attitude toward money.

Jed needed a team. The reality is, *your Millionaire Maker plan defines your team.* Who joins first depends on where you need immediate assistance. If you want to establish a business entity first, then your top goal is to get an entity specialist. If assets are first—say, for example, you want to transfer the equity in your house to usable cash—then a mortgage broker gets a quick call. If, like Jed, you need to learn about a variety of areas, then mentors are your first step. You might consider successful entrepreneurs to give you thoughts on how you can earn more money and investors to help you with assets. Jed's Millionaire Maker plan relied on his collecting a huge amount of information on a number of subjects.

Based on my suggestion that he pursue small-risk, small-reward investments just to get started, Jed decided to learn the fundamentals of the due diligence checklist by investing in some stocks. This did not mean giving his money to a broker to invest or throwing his cash into mutual funds. This meant researching companies to learn about their fundamentals. Public companies are required to share their financials, so they're a good place to start.

In his search for a good mentor, Jed sought out the father of a friend who was a portfolio manager at a bank in Boston and asked him to lunch. To prepare for the meeting, Jed read books on stock valuation and scoured several investing sites on the Internet. After lunch, he asked the portfolio manager to introduce him to other bankers, stock analysts, and some high-net-worth individuals, emphasizing that these meetings were purely for informational and educational purposes.

> *Leading one's wealth means knowing one's highest and best use of time.*

Eventually, these meetings had an extra bonus. Not only did Jed meet wealthy individuals who knew how to find and value assets, but he endeared himself to them by asking them to continue in a mentoring capacity with him. And it was these relationships that, in a few years, gave Jed access to real deal flow.

Jed also asked these mentors for referrals of accountants, lawyers, and even a personal bookkeeper so that he did not have to spend his time doing what he could hire someone else to do for just $20 an hour. Leading one's wealth means knowing one's *highest and best use of time.* For Jed, doing his own books wasn't it.

Because Jed did not have a lot of money to start with, he made a point of learning how to use OPM. By leveraging his money with others, he could participate in bigger and better deals. Further on in the book, you'll see how Jed used his mentors and OPM to get into some higher-risk, higher-reward games.

Type 2: Saving to Delay Spending

Saving is delayed spending. Money can't sit around and be expected to make you wealthy. You have to put it to work. Allison Connor was a psychologist in southern Florida making $40,000 annually. Newly married, Allison and her husband rented a small apartment. He was in graduate school studying architecture on a full scholarship, with a

___

Saving is delayed spending.

___

stipend that covered his books. They had no credit card debt, but they barely managed to stay ahead of their expenses on just her salary. Any extra money that Allison did have went into her mutual funds and an IRA. But she and her husband wanted to start a family, and Allison knew that she wouldn't be able to keep up the hours she worked once that happened. She had it in her head that she needed to find a way to create "mailbox money," those cash-flow checks that come into your mailbox every month.

Allison's Gap Analysis looked like this:

FREEDOM DAY GOALS

- *$500,000 in invested assets*
- *$5,000/month passive income*
- *A nice home in Florida*

- *Fewer hours at work*
- *Manage debt*

REVENUE	ASSETS

FINANCIAL BASELINE

PRETAX INCOME: *$3,333/MONTH*	ASSETS:	*$10,000**
EXPENDITURES: *$1,500/MONTH*	LIABILITIES:	*$0*
	NET WORTH:	*$10,000*

*$6,000 in mutual funds; $4,000 in IRAs
SKILL SET: problem solving, communication, management.

Like Jed Stone, Allison needed to make more money. But first, she needed to move her extra income into a Wealth Account and away from lazy assets. Unlike Jed, Allison was good at managing her expenses, and she would probably increase the funds in her Wealth Account pretty quickly. This would get her into assets sooner rather than later.

Early in her wealth-building efforts, Allison found a mentor who had invested in several Laundromats in the Florida area. She was intrigued and amused by the idea of consumers constantly feeding coins into her bank account. After establishing a Wealth Account, Allison focused on making more money with a side business. Her Cash Machine was a Web site directory of psychologists for stay-at-home mothers who needed a quick phone consultation. It took three months to build word of mouth, but soon she was doubling the amount of funds she had available for investing in her Wealth Account. Marketing was a key element in this acceleration. Most inexperienced entrepreneurs don't plan, budget, or focus enough to have a successful marketing plan, but Allison focused heavily on the marketing, and her volume grew. Thanks to her limited liability company and her capacity to run her earnings through it, she was retaining more of that income. In Chapter 12, on alternative assets, I'll take you through Allison's process for getting into Laundromats.

Type 3: Restructuring Assets

Mick and Mary Buchanan were living close to the bone. Even though he made $120,000 a year as a marketing consultant in Dallas and she earned $30,000 annually managing a pet shop, little of that money seemed to make its way home after taxes. They'd bought their house five years previously and had about $200,000 in equity in it. They also had money in mutual funds; they had an IRA, and there was some money in Mick's 401(k). But they never had enough money to do much, always had a balance on their credit cards, and had little put away in their children's college account. Mick wanted to quit working and run a fishing charter company in the Caribbean. Mary was right there with him.

Mick's Gap Analysis looked like this:

FREEDOM DAY GOALS

- $1,000,000 in invested assets
- $10,000/month passive income
- Kids' college paid for

- Charter boat fishing company
- No job for Mary or Mick

REVENUE	ASSETS

FINANCIAL BASELINE

PRETAX INCOME: $12,500/MONTH
EXPENDITURES: $8,000/MONTH

ASSETS: $590,000
LIABILITIES: $304,000
NET WORTH: $286,000

- $500,000 value of home
- $40,000 in mutual funds
- $25,000 in 401(k)
- $21,000 in IRA
- $4,000 in bank

- $300,000 mortgage on the house
- $4,000 credit card debt

SKILL SET: marketing, budgeting, organization.

The Buchanans were living a poorly managed life. Mick was *committed to the commute*. And the guy was barely breaking even for his efforts. He was a marketing consultant, yet he hadn't properly structured his business with entities that would help him retain much of his income. The Buchanans needed to keep more of the money they made and start building up wealth.

Mick immediately set up a business entity and began channeling his revenue and expenditures through the entity. After that, he was ready to start looking at restructuring his assets. He was willing to take $100,000 out of the equity of his home, as well as the $40,000 from his mutual funds, to invest in other assets. He got involved in some cash-flow-producing real estate properties, much like what you'll see when we discuss our cash-poor millionaire. But Mick was most interested in private business ventures. While the money from his consultancy fed his Wealth Account, Mick began scouting out other opportunities. His first step into private equity involved a private-label nutritional products manufacturing and distribution business. He also began to support his wealth creation by making more money and better managing his credit card debt.

Type 4: The Cash-Poor Millionaire

When I met Dee Newton she was 54, living in Santa Monica, California, divorced, with two kids in high school, and vice president of information technology at a large health-care company.

Dee was an example of someone with badly invested assets. Though prudent, Dee said that her household and family expenses, including her car lease and mortgage interest, were at least $4,000 a month. Before taxes, her income was $6,000 a month; she barely broke even and had to cover some of her monthly expenses with credit cards. Dee's house was her biggest asset. She'd bought it 10 years ago for $300,000, and the housing market in Santa Monica had skyrocketed. Her home had recently been appraised for $1 million.

Dee's Gap Analysis looked like this:

FREEDOM DAY GOALS

- *$3,000,000 in invested assets*
- *$30,000/month passive cash flow*
- *Kids' college tuition plan in place*

- *Fund for $1 million in charitable gifts*
- *Millionaire Maker portfolios for the kids*
- *Manage debt*

REVENUE	ASSETS

FINANCIAL BASELINE

PRETAX INCOME: $6,000/MONTH
EXPENDITURES: $4,000/MONTH

ASSETS:	$1,220,000
LIABILITIES:	$216,000
NET WORTH:	$1,004,000

- *$1,000,000 value of home*
- *$60,000 in stocks and bonds*
- *$70,000 in 401(k)*
- *$80,000 in IRA*
- *$10,000 in bank*

- *$200,000 mortgage on the house*
- *$16,000 credit card debt*

SKILL SET: *management, organization, budgeting, communication, health-care knowledge.*

Many people would claim that with a net worth of $1,004,000, Dee was in great shape. And they'd be wrong.

Dee's financial well-being was an illusion. She was a classic case of the cash-poor millionaire. To someone with nothing, this might seem like a good problem to have. But unless cash-poor millionaires can sell their assets and change their lifestyles, that money represents golden handcuffs. In order for Dee to have any real cash in her pocket, she needed to sell her assets, inevitably eroding any wealth she had. Since houses in the city in which she lived had enjoyed such great appreciation, Dee might consider cashing out her house, but then she would need to

1. Spend at least the value of her old house to get something similar

2. Get a smaller house *or*

3. Move to another, maybe less appealing, area

Dee didn't like any of these choices, especially since her current district had excellent public schools. She wasn't eager to exchange living expenses for private school tuition.

In summary, Dee had badly invested assets, no extra cash coming in, no business entities, and no forecasting or tax strategies to help her retain more income. Like too many of us, Dee Newton was building up a whole lot of nothing financially. She needed to generate real cash flow and continue to grow her net worth.

The first step, then, was to restructure some of her assets. Dee's assets of $1,220,000 consisted of

- $1,000,000 value of her home, $800,000 of which was equity
- $60,000 in stocks and bonds
- $70,000 in 401(k)
- $80,000 in IRAs
- $10,000 cash in the bank

I talked to Dee about what she was willing to do with these assets. But first, I needed to help her understand how to turn them into more effective ones and create a corporate structure to protect these new assets. This is one of the first items in the Wealth Cycle Investing Worksheet:

—Setup—			
Source of Funds			
Wealth Account	OPM*	Debt/Bank Loan	Restructuring of Other Assets
Entities			
Forecasting			

Dee's source of funds would be the restructuring of other assets. But while it's one thing to say you want to get a home equity loan or do a refinancing, it's another thing to know the best way to do it.

Loans and Refinancing

Loans and refinancing are where team building begins. A smart, experienced, and creative mortgage broker was a terrific first player to join Dee's team. Leading your wealth starts with finding competent and informed advisors and facilitators.

Taking cash out of your assets is not difficult, and the benefits of converting a lazy asset into an energized one are worth the time, effort, and—okay, let's call it what it is—paperwork that you have to do. As I said, the choice is yours: You can do paperwork, or you can be poor. If your due diligence efforts are effective,

You can do paperwork, or you can be poor.

you can still keep your nest egg relatively safe—only now it will generate healthy returns. It bears repeating: Risk is the failure to educate yourself about an opportunity. Risk is reduced by knowing the right people in the right deals and collecting the best information you can about both. Chances are you have the key ingredient to get information and help; it's called desire.

Once you have gotten the help and done the research, you're in control, and no one else should be. With the equity converted and cash in hand, the number of assets in which you can invest is endless. But, the number of good ones is not. Picking through the pile to find the good deals is your responsibility. You must strive to gain access to the best deals and then, once you find them, select the ones that are best for you.

IRAs

IRAs are another source of funds. Many investors have found that the typical response to the idea of using IRA money for real estate or oil and gas investments is that it can't be done. Well, when I hear *no,* I say *next.* That means that you go to another accountant or advisor—one who has a solution and who wants to be creative about helping you reach your goals. The firms that stick to the old model tend to suggest that qualified money move only into stocks, bonds, or mutual funds. This keeps the money in-house, that is, in their house.

> *The good deals are out there, and with help from your team, you will find them.*

However, there are several firms that will help you take your IRA, or a 401(k) from a company that you no longer work for and that you can access, and put it into alternative assets. Usually, these are more progressive firms that understand nontraditional assets. Deal flow needs cash flow. That means that those with deals to do need money to do them. There's always demand for your money, and if you cater to that demand, you can put your money to work and make more money. I've found that the best brokerage firms will help you make money with your IRA. They will help you reduce your risk and increase your reward by working with you to find investment opportunities for this money across a full range of assets.

It is worth taking the time and energy to find such firms. By using tax-deferred IRA money or tax-free Roth IRA cash, you can accelerate your wealth, as these structures allow you to retain that money on a tax-deferred basis—and withdraw it tax free. You can also partner with your own IRA, so that in an investment, both you personally and your IRA can benefit, as you split up profits and expenses in a way that will maximize tax benefits. IRAs can be used to invest in several different types of assets, such as real estate, real estate options, accounts receivable factoring, or promissory notes. This allows you

Deal flow needs cash flow.

to enjoy interest payments that are tax free. True self-directed IRAs are few and far between. You may find it hard to discover a custodian firm that really understands the type of asset allocation we're doing in the Wealth Cycle.

Entities

Before I presented specific assets to Dee, we went over how she'd restructure her life into a *corporate* life. Dee researched the companies she'd need to set up. To begin with, she'd create a limited liability company (LLC) for her investment vehicles and a trust to serve as an umbrella for all of her companies and holdings.

You might be thinking that this requires doing a lot of research and paperwork that is not very exciting. I'll say it again: *You can do paperwork, or you can be poor.* Once you find an expert in entity structuring, you will be surprised how easy it is to set these up. Information on entities—what it means to have a company versus a corporation versus a partnership versus a trust—is available in publications and on the Internet. It's important that you do this research before you ask an accountant for help. While there are thousands of great accountants out there who fully understand entity structuring, far too many do not. If you do not know the right questions to ask based on your research, you will not get the best answers. A primer on entities is available in *The Millionaire Maker,* and a directory of terrific accountants and entity specialists is listed on www.liveoutloud.com.

I offer these references for one reason only: I'm not a fan of theory or concepts. Wealth Cycle Investing is contingent on action. You must take action in order to be successful. If I just talk about a team but don't tell you how to get one, or if I just suggest certain asset allocations but don't spell out for you how I did it, then I'm being interesting but not helpful. On the Live Out Loud Web site, look for the section on Assets Education and you'll find help on most of the topics discussed in this book, or speak to one of our strategists—they'll answer your questions and help get you going. The goal is to get you moving in the right direction as soon as possible.

Creating entities, such as an LLC, allowed Dee to properly account for the revenue and expenditures associated with these investments. Forecasting was essential for Dee to maximize her income through tax benefits. (For example, Dee could expense the portion of her car lease used to drive to oil and gas investor meetings and make due diligence trips.)

Money Rules

Before we could figure out which assets were the best for Dee, she and I had to establish her Money Rules. In the Wealth Cycle Investing Worksheet, they read as follows:

—MONEY RULES—		
ROI GOAL AND PROJECTED		
CASH FLOW		APPRECIATION
ACTIVE		PASSIVE
DIVERSIFICATION		
Allocation	Risk/Reward	Exit Strategy

ROI Goal and Projected

Dee's Freedom Day goals were to have $3 million in invested assets, $30,000 per month in passive cash flow, her kids' college tuition plans in place, a fund for $1 million in charitable gifts, and her debt under control. In order to have $30,000 a month in passive income, Dee would need to achieve an ROI of 12 percent on her eventual $3 million in invested assets. Given that in the beginning she'd only have a fraction of that amount in invested assets, we'd look for investments with projected ROIs in the range of 20 to 30 percent to help her accelerate her assets.

Cash Flow and Appreciation

Because her initial goal was to increase her passive income, Dee started by looking for cash-flow assets. *Cash-flow assets* are investments that produce monthly passive income, such as rent from a real estate holding, interest on a promissory note, or a dividend from a business. Appreciating assets are investments that may increase in value over time. They include real estate in growing markets and businesses that focus on growth.

Active versus Passive

Although Dee would always invest directly in each asset, she would have to decide, for each investment, if she wanted to be an active or a passive investor. Active investors are directly involved in the asset and contribute significantly to day-to-day operations. Passive investors trust the current leadership or management team and place their dollars like votes for these people.

Diversification

By looking at diversification and the risk/reward assessment, I can also determine the kind of balance the portfolio has and needs. In

Dee's case, most of her asset value was centered on one appreciating asset, her house. She needed to diversify into more cash-flow assets and other asset classes. Given her initial ROI goal of 20 to 30 percent, we would be pretty aggressive in the risk/reward bucket.

The exit strategy is an important component of asset selection in that it affects your diversification and your tax strategy. If all your assets are ballooning appreciation investments waiting for a big hit at the end of five years, that's not diversification, and it will have a negative impact on your taxes. (We'll continue to cover this in Chapter 4, "Money Rules.")

To get started, Dee was willing to use $300,000 of her $1,220,000 for direct asset allocation. This came from the following sources:

- $220,000 from the equity in her home
- $40,000 from some underperforming mutual funds
- $40,000 from her IRAs, which she moved over into a true self-directed IRA

Dee was not in a position to leave her job, so the money in the 401(k) stayed put. With refinancing, she now had a $410,000 mortgage on which she'd be paying 8 percent, adding $1,500 to her monthly expenses. Since we both felt that she could make more than 8 percent on her investments, restructuring made sense. She was borrowing money at a rate that was less than the projected return on her assets. My wealth team and I helped Dee consider a diverse range of unconventional and aggressive income-generating assets for this money.

Team

It was now time for the next part of the worksheet, identifying resources for attaining knowledge.

—*TEAM*—

LEADER:

FIELD PARTNER:

MENTOR(s):

PROFESSIONALS:
  Entity Specialist
  Accountant
  Bookkeeper
  Lawyer

UTILITY PLAYERS:
  Help at work
  Help at home

PARTNERS AND COLLEAGUES:

To execute these deals, I needed to call on my community of wealth builders. You can't do this on your own; you need a team. Members of your wealth-building team will share their experience and expertise, their industry knowledge, deal information, and, many times, the capital or credit to get the deal done. Finding and building this community is your goal, and it is the key to your success in building your Wealth Cycle.

You will use your team, as I did, to keep learning, changing, and growing. Think about the worlds of people you know from childhood or school or former jobs. Chances are that many of them have capital, contacts, expertise, and energy. Gather these people together and start to build your community. If you do not know any such people personally, seek out established wealth-building communities of which you can become a part. Remember, it is just as important to have

> **It is just as important to have good people on your side as to have good investments.**

good people on your side as to have good investments. It is imperative that you allow only positive, honest, good people into your world. This means that if your Uncle Joe is nice, but negative, he's out. If your friend Ben from work is always fighting with everyone over the smallest issues, he's out. If your lawyer once shared a story of how he got the best of someone, he's out. *Do not* bring bad company into your community. And if you find that such people have made their way into it somehow, get them out, fast. You're looking for positive, credible, ethical, courageous, enthusiastic, generous people.

Do not bring bad company into your team.

In order to find the right investments for Dee, I called on

1. An entrepreneur from one of my Big Tables, which are networks of investors who help one another create and find deals. This entrepreneur was buying and restructuring a private-label nutritional products manufacturing and distribution business that was already producing annual cash flows of 30 percent on capital. I'd done extensive due diligence on this deal and was in it myself.

2. A colleague of mine who was coordinating promissory notes for people he knew who needed hard-money loans. The going rate was 12 percent. Once you build or find your world of wealth builders, this is an excellent source of income for those with capital, and a great source of capital for those with an idea. These types of transactions rely exclusively on trust and transparency, which means that both the borrower and the lender must be clear about the deal, have a legal contract, and share full information. In my community of wealth builders, we have zero tolerance for

anyone who is not honest and open about deals. Our rule is, "One strike and you're out."

3. A field partner of mine in a bread-and-butter state who was willing to sell Dee (at a profit for himself, of course) 10 cash-flow-producing houses.

4. An energy entrepreneur who had extensive experience in oil and gas and had a company that allowed investors to diversify their dollars over several wells for a less risky shot at great returns, as well as depreciation benefits.

5. Another field partner of mine who was doing some land/preconstruction real estate deals in a southern state that had projected appreciation.

Each of these connections would be part of a specific team for that asset and was listed at the top of the worksheet.

| ASSET UNDER CONSIDERATION: |
| CONTACT PERSON(S): |

Again, these deals were all identified through a wealth-building community. Though putting together a network like this may seem difficult, it's not. You'd be surprised at how quickly you can build a similar web of wealth builders. I've given advice to hundreds of clients who want to build their own network, and I am always pleased to see how quickly these communities are built and how fast they take off. It's important to understand that almost every net-work or community hits some development bumps along the way. I sure did. But despite inevitable growing pains, building and maintaining a team is well worth the effort.

Note that two of the opportunities presented to Dee—the nutritional products manufacturer and oil and gas—are deals that are open only to accredited investors. These are, as we said, individuals who have

> *Despite inevitable growing pains, building and maintaining a team is well worth the effort*

a net worth of $1 million, who meet the income minimum, or who have the trust requirement. Dee, boosted by the value of her house, met the million-dollar net worth criterion. As a point of clarification, home equity counts toward net worth only when an investor is considering a private offering. If Dee were considering a public offering, she would not meet the accredited investor requirement because she would not be able to apply her home equity toward her net worth.

Due Diligence

It was one thing for Dee to hear about deals, but it was her responsibility to make the decision to do them or not. Performing due diligence would be the most important factor in Dee's investment decision.

—DUE DILIGENCE—				
DATA	DISCUSSION	DISCOVERY	DIAGNOSIS	DECISION

Due diligence is covered extensively in Chapter 6. Briefly, due diligence begins with collecting information through a team. The team should help you find data, get into the discussion, kick the tires through discovery, and make a diagnosis for the final decision. Your team is involved in the entire process, but the final yes or no on the investment is always your responsibility.

Subject to due diligence, Dee's asset plan looked like this:

FREEDOM DAY GOALS

- *$3,000,000 in invested assets*
- *$30,000/month passive flow*
- *Kids' college tuition plan in place*
- *Fund for $1 million in charitable gifts*
- *Millionaire Maker portfolios for the kids*
- *Manage debt*

REVENUE	ASSETS
PASSIVE INCOME CASH FLOW:	**$300,000 SHIFT OF ASSETS:**
$1,750/month cash flow: start-up	*$70,000 into a start-up company with 30 percent annual yield*
$450/month cash flow: promissary note	
$2,000/month cash flow: houses	*$45,000 promissory note at 12 percent annual yield*
Total passive income: $4,200	
	$60,000 in 10 bread-and-butter cash-flow houses that require $6,000 cash each to acquire, including closing costs, and create $200 a month each in cash flow.
EVENTUAL PASSIVE INCOME:	
After 18 months, $3,000/month cash flow	
	$100,000 in 50 oil and gas wells. After 18 months ramp-up, given probability of wells that will hit, this can create 3 percent cash flow a month.
APPRECIATION: *(from preconstruction)*	
$28,000 year 1, 12 percent growth	
$33,000 year 2, 19 percent growth	*$25,000 in two preconstruction houses*

FINANCIAL BASELINE

PRETAX INCOME: $10,200/MONTH

EXPENDITURES: $5,500/MONTH

ASSETS:	$1,440,000
LIABILITIES:	$436,000
NET WORTH:	$1,004,000

- *Pretax income per month increased immediately by $4,200.*
- *Amount of assets and liabilities increased by the amount of debt we borrowed, $220,000, while the net worth, before Dee realized any appreciation, stayed the same.*
- *Monthly expenditures, not yet allowing for depreciation deductions, increased by $1,500 for the 8 percent interest due on the new equity loan.*

To clarify the housing deal, the 10 cash-flow-producing bread-and-butter houses were each worth $45,000. The $6,000 for each covered a 10 percent down payment, $4,500, plus $1,500 for closing costs. The rent on the property was $695, and the PITI (principal, interest, taxes, and insurance) plus the equity line payment for the refinancing and management fees equaled $495. The remainder was the $200-a-month cash flow. These numbers will vary depending on the investor's credit rating and other factors. These are great cash-flow-producing assets, but we limited the investment to 10 houses in order to diversify Dee's asset allocation.

This shift in assets gave Dee

1. Passive income of $4,200 per month just from a small shift of her assets, which put her well on her way to an eventual $10,000 a month, especially once the oil and gas investments ramped up.
2. Appreciating assets of $25,000.
3. Depreciation against passive income on the real estate assets and an intangible drilling cost deduction against ordinary income on the gas and oil investments. These are expenditures against revenue, which would also allow Dee to pay less in taxes and retain more of that revenue.
4. The basis upon which to create entities that would help Dee retain more of her income.

The Before and After

By doing just a small part of what she could do with her assets, Dee

- Almost doubled her monthly income
- Began to pay off and better manage her credit card debt

- Contributed to plans for her children's college tuition
- Started creating multiple streams of income from appreciating and cash-generating assets, in which she could also involve her children as employees to teach them about the Wealth Cycle

Next Steps

Dee set up two Wealth Accounts, one for personal use and one as a holding account in her LLC into which the passive income would flow and later be used to fund more assets. By making consistent and simultaneous payments into her Wealth Accounts and being diligent about a debt elimination plan, Dee's wealth building would resolve her credit card debt. Additional cash would be set aside for tax-free educational savings accounts to allow Dee to pay her children's college tuition with pretax dollars.

To accelerate the Wealth Cycle and continue to generate more assets, Dee knew that she could make more money with her own business, which would allow her to set up more entities and retain more cash. And, if she decided to make additional real estate investments, it would be in her best interest to leave her current W-2 job to enjoy the full depreciation benefits of those investments—a benefit that is available only to real estate professionals.

Unless a person is a real estate professional, as designated by the IRS, that person is limited to $25,000 in depreciation deductions, and even that goes away when adjusted gross income exceeds $150,000. That means that if a person has real estate that generates $100,000 in depreciation, but refuses to leave his or her job, then that person is losing $75,000 in deductible dollars to stay committed to the commute. That seems like a poor trade-off. And although the passive losses aren't gone forever, because they can be carried forward until they are used up or until the property gets sold, I've seen too many investors lose this because they do in fact exit the investment before they have carried forward the expenditures.

Dee, with a new commitment to leading her wealth, reconditioned the way she viewed money, and now, with her team, was in charge of her wealth.

Like Dee Newton, each of the investors mentioned in this chapter got into assets. I'll show you how they did these deals. It all begins with establishing and understanding your Money Rules.

Money Rules

Taking Control

When you opt for direct participation in assets, you need to make decisions based on your personal criteria—your Money Rules. Your Money Rules are determined by your current situation and financial objectives, and they help you decide

1. Which investments to make
2. How to make them
3. What you need to do to get started
4. Whom to involve

Your Current Situation and Financial Objectives

If you're raising three kids, working two jobs, and juggling mortgages, then the needs of your current situation are a bit different from the considerations of those who have no such responsibilities. If you have a lot of necessary expenditures, then you need to consider cash-flow-producing assets immediately. Appreciation is no friend of yours at this point. Sometimes we tend to regard net worth as the be-all and the end-all. But that's just an accounting number. Net worth doesn't mean much if you don't have cold hard cash in your pocket to buy the essentials of daily life. If, on the other hand, your Financial Baseline reveals a current situation where there is enough cash coming in, then you might want to focus on appreciation.

As you establish your goals and your Freedom Day, it's important to have your mind focused on the bigger picture or long-term vision. This vision will become the driving force that gets you through everyday hurdles and motivates you beyond your short-term goals. While you might experience a bit of adrenaline as you pay down your debt and start to accumulate assets in the Wealth Cycle, it will be the overall vision that keeps you on the path to reaching millionaire status.

When you engage in the Wealth Cycle, you employ *no-limit thinking*. This means that you stretch. A vision is big—really big. And if your vision doesn't scare you even a little bit, it's not big enough.

Once you know where you are and where you want to go, you have the criteria—the Money Rules—that will inform your investment decisions and be the compass that keeps you on track. Without them, you are susceptible to possible weakness in your resolve along the way and the unpredictability of the markets on any given day. You must protect your wealth against unknowns. Money Rules free you from emotional impulses and offer the objectivity you need when evaluating deals.

The Money Rules section of the worksheet looks like this:

—Money Rules—		
ROI Goal and Projected		
Cash Flow		Appreciation
Active		Passive
Diversification		
Allocation	Risk/Reward	Exit Strategy

ROI Goal and Projected

In order to hit your short- and long-term goals, it's important to find assets that satisfy your needs and objectives for the targeted ROI with regard to both cash-flow requirements and appreciation targets. Each time you visit the assets building block you will determine the amount of money you have available for making investments and how much you need to earn from those investments in order for them to be worthwhile.

An investment is worthwhile if it is a better vehicle for wealth creation than simply keeping your cash in the bank. This type of relativity is how many investors consider the value of an investment. For example, if the banks are offering a 5 percent interest rate, you want the return on your investment to exceed that rate. Then it's important to assess the risk that comes with that return. If you find an asset that will give you a 6 percent return on your investment, but there's only a one-out-of-ten chance that the return is going to happen, then that's too much risk for such a small reward—especially when you can get 5 percent in a bank account. In order to become a millionaire in a short period of time, you can't accept these single-digit returns. They just won't get you there fast enough. *The objective is to find high-reward, double-digit returns with direct asset allocation investments and minimize the risk with education, knowledge, a team, and due diligence.*

Using leverage with investments is another way to improve your ROI. Let's say, for example, that you are investing directly in an asset that offers you a 10 percent return on that investment. If you buy it for all cash, then your cash-on-cash return is 10 percent. But if you have to invest only a portion of the cash needed, your return will be higher. For example, if you invest $100,000 cash to buy a real estate property that delivers a 10 percent return, you'll get $10,000—again, a cash-on-cash return of 10 percent. But let's say you put in only a $20,000 cash down payment and borrow the rest. You still get $10,000 on the $100,000 total investment, but your ROI on your $20,000 cash is 50 percent, less the interest payments you made on the $80,000 you borrowed for the investment. Whether getting a mortgage on real estate, buying stocks on margin, or using OPM (other people's money) to help finance a deal, using leverage gets you a higher return on your cash investment—provided the asset appreciates.

One word of caution here around using leverage: it multiplies your reward when an investment goes up and your risk when it goes down. For example, if the same $100,000 piece of real estate went down by 10 percent, you would have lost $10,000—or half of the $20,000 cash you invested in the deal. That's a negative 50 percent ROI. Successful wealth builders use leverage wisely by always considering the down-side risk in a deal. Never take on more leverage than you can handle if things don't work out as planned.

As you can see in the Wealth Cycle Investing Worksheet, there are two ROI numbers that we look at, goal and projected. The goal ROI is the return that you need your money to make to reach a certain objective. The projected ROI is the potential return on any given investment.

In Dee Newton's case, she had $1,220,000 in assets and was looking for $10,000 passive income a month, which meant that Dee needed to achieve an ROI of 10 percent. Investments with potential ROIs in the 8 to 12 percent range would meet her goals. But if you're starting with nothing, like Jed Stone, or if you want your Wealth Cycle to move faster, you need to participate in higher-return investments to build assets. After getting a handle on the fundamentals of investing, collecting knowledge, and getting a team, Jed would look for potential ROIs in the double digits.

In some cases, the potential ROI is an accurate indicator of what the actual ROI will be. For example, if you're investing in a mobile home park with a team that's overseen the homes for a few years now, and if the park has reliable property managers, minimal repair and upkeep fees, and steady demand, and the homes cost $10,000 down and when rented offer $100 a month income, there's a good chance that you will see that 12 percent annual ROI. But for many investments ROI is a speculative number, and one has to allow for the risk associated with that speculation. Knowledge of the asset, the market in which it competes, and the management and trust in your field partner can help minimize the risk and keep the ROI intact. That's why these factors are essential in making choices about investments and why I insist on getting a team that maintains control.

Cash Flow and/or Appreciation

Depending on the range of ROI you're seeking to earn, you need to decide if that ROI is going to contribute to your income strategy or your growth strategy. If income, you will select assets that provide monthly or quarterly cash flow. Income investors want money that's coming into their mailboxes every month or every quarter. They want to see dividends on stocks, cash flow from rental properties, or distributions from private equity. Debt instruments, such as promissory notes, are good examples of this type of fixed-income vehicle. Income-generating real estate properties and oil wells are others.

Some people don't want or need more income and are looking only for appreciation, or growth. Land on the edge of suburban sprawl, for example, real estate properties in booming areas, and many new business ventures often promise growth. Growth investors want to see annual numbers, such as sales and market share, that do one thing: go up. They don't care if they see any of the money right away. Growth investors aren't interested in cash flow or dividends; they want all of the excess cash to feed the business in the form of retained earnings so that it can continue to grow. They get involved in markets where the asset has the potential to hit on trends and where they can patiently ride the currents to bigger numbers sometime in the future.

Many investors who are looking for growth are also value investors. You may well find that this perspective helps you identify better growth vehicles. Value investors look for investments at a discount. They look for the undiscovered diamond in the rough, invest in it, watch it burst out into maturity, and take the profits. I always think of value investors as optimistic parents; they see something that no one else sees, and they are willing to put a long-term focus on it. Value investors use comparable analysis when deciding which investments they think are available at a discount. They analyze several assets in one class and compare metrics, such as sales and earnings. If they find that one of these assets has strong metrics but is priced lower than its comparables by the public or private markets, then the value investor will consider this a good buy. Being a value investor is a lot more art than science, though, because many times the asset is perceived and priced as a laggard for good reason. There is always the chance, however, that something is being overlooked.

Then there are those investors who look for vehicles that provide both income and growth. Individuals who seek out income investments are just looking for fixed income—something that they can rely on. But there are also those who look for aggressive income generators, assets that they hope might also give them some appreciation too as icing on the cake. An up-and-running business venture that's being recalibrated for improvements can create both immediate dividends and appreciation. If these vehicles fit your current needs and objectives, they can be a boon to your portfolio. For some who don't want the annual tax implications of that extra income and don't have tax strategies to deal with it, growth alone is often enough.

Neither cash flow nor appreciation investments—or the combination of the two—are difficult to find, but the investor must be specific in his or her intention. Investors who just look at various investments, without an objective for growth, income, or a combined opportunity, won't find the deals that are right for them. To become a millionaire investor, you need a plan—a plan that you stick to. Most investors do not fall into one single category. Those who

> *To become a millionaire investor, you need to stick to a plan.*

have committed to the Wealth Cycle method have elements of all three types, depending on the mix they want to bring to their Millionaire Maker portfolio.

Active or Passive

Whether they are active or passive investors, Wealth Cycle investors never abdicate control. An active investor is one who is very involved in the asset and, as a result, may take on some additional risk. The active investor may be a general partner, manager, director, consultant, or advisor. A passive investor delivers capital and trusts the general partners, management, directors, and advisors to deliver the projected returns on that investment. It's important to note that in our model, passive does not mean removed. In Wealth Cycle Investing, you are never distanced from your investments.

In both cases, the investor must keep an eye on the investment. Sometimes it's easier for passive investors to do that because they can remain objective. And sometimes it's easier for active investors to do that because they can actually get into the ongoing business activities and move things in the right direction. Either way, investors have their specific responsibilities, and if the appropriate checks and balances are in place, both types of investors are properly served.

You must make the decision to be active or passive in any deal before the investment is formalized. This way, everyone is clear on his or her role and responsibilities, and the degree to which he or she can drive the outcome. The decision to be active or passive on a specific deal depends on your time, energy, capacity, skill set, and experience. Many people are both, actively running one investment and investing passively in others for good diversification.

Diversification

As most experienced investors know, it's not *if* one of your deals will tank, but *when*. For that reason, it's hard to find an investing book that doesn't recommend diversification, and I fully support diversification as a strategy. Diversification, though, is a term that is often misunderstood. The point of diversification is to minimize risk, maximize reward, and protect yourself from the vulnerability of any one investment. To do this, investors distribute their money over a range of opportunities. The misunderstanding occurs when investors think they're diversifying by investing a little bit in a lot of different assets, but that is not a good diversification strategy.

A good strategy is to consider different assets, then seek out diversification within the asset class or classes on which you've chosen to focus. I'm diverse in that I like to buy into different types of assets, such as oil and gas, real estate, and business ventures. Then, within those asset classes, I buy several different opportunities. For instance, I like to buy oil and gas, and I like to be directly involved. As I've mentioned, I do not buy oil and gas stocks; I buy privately offered shares of the actual wells. But I don't buy one or two shares of one or two wells. I buy hundreds of shares of hundreds of wells.

Traditionally oil and gas is a high-risk, high-reward investment, with only a handful of wells performing. But those winners can earn a ton of money—even after paying for the losers. If you buy a share of just one well, your probability of success is low. But if you buy shares in 10 wells, or better yet 20 wells, or even better 100 wells, then you've just diversified your investment within an asset class and given yourself a much higher probability of success.

There are also investors who prefer to really get to know just one asset class. That's fine as long as they diversify by buying into several different opportunities within that class. Real estate offers many opportunities for diversification within an asset class. One is to buy both cash-flow and appreciating assets. Another is geographic diversification. By investing in different towns and states, you can hedge your bets against the booms and busts that may occur in various regions. Still another good diversification strategy in real estate is to purchase a variety of property types, for example, commercial, multifamily, single family, and so on.

Your strategy should also include diversifying yields. Some investors have one group of assets with yields in the 20 to 30 percent range, some at the 15 percent level, and then some long-term holdings at the under 10 percent level. Because risk and reward are closely tied, diversifying your reward is another way of diversifying your risk.

Diversifying the length of time you hold various assets is a good idea also. If the exit strategies for your assets all hit on the same date, they're all going to be susceptible to the same economic climate, whether that's good or bad. Not to mention that you'll have quite a tax issue. You should also diversify your investing strategy, managing a combination of cash-flow producers, appreciation assets, active investments, and passive investments. And you should have some high-risk, high-reward assets and some lower-risk, lower-reward investments. You can also balance your portfolio with a little equity (ownership for long-term payout) and a little debt (loans with short-term interest coming your way).

As you look at investments, keep in mind that there are a lot of different opportunities out there. Some are conventional and traditional; others are brand new and innovative. Some represent huge companies and markets; others are small and unfolding. Some are domestic; some are global. By considering more opportunities, you are diversifying your portfolio. It is also a good idea to include capital-intensive assets, which are assets that have property or equipment that is depreciated over time, to realize paper expenses from that depreciation, which can offset some of the revenue.

Diversification also allows you to be more flexible. Conviction is an important step in being committed to becoming a millionaire, but it doesn't mean that you have to stand by your mistakes. The economic environment is a fluid thing, susceptible to world events, the human condition, and all sorts of micro and macro possibilities. Too many times I've seen perfectly sound assets take a hit from volatile events that surround them. For this reason, it is imperative that you always stay on your toes and be ready to pivot when the moment calls for it. Results are what you're looking for, and that means good returns. If an asset seemed appealing, but is eking out only a little cash and growth is flat, the investor must be flexible and real-locate that investment to another asset. A diverse portfolio means that you're not locked into a single asset, so you won't be as vulnerable to the ups and

A diverse portfolio means that you're not locked into a single asset, so you won't be as vulnerable to the ups and downs that every category experiences.

downs that every category experiences. Flexibility, awareness, and adaptability are the underappreciated attributes of any good diver-sification strategy. Though you must remain committed to the overall vision, each choice in your strategy should be consistently evaluated and reallocated as it becomes necessary. Your strategy will be systematic and sure, and you will move decisively and delib-erately. But when things are bad, you must realize that there is no reward in suffering. Because you are in control, you have the lux-ury of getting out and moving on. This is all a part of diversifica-tion, allocation, and risk/reward maintenance.

To control a diverse portfolio, you need a team. It's essential for you to work with others because you cannot do it all expertly your-self. Diversifying your portfolio so that it includes different types of assets takes a good amount of research. This doesn't mean that you have to do all of this research yourself. You should do some of it and oversee everything, but you also can hire researchers or include due diligence professionals, lawyers, and analysts on your team. There are even companies that focus exclusively on conducting due dili-gence for investors. The final decision is still your responsibility, but it can be very helpful to have others gather and collect some of the information with you.

Remember: you have to lead your wealth, but you don't have to do everything yourself.

The Wealth Cycle Connection

To drive home the importance of Wealth Cycle Investing's interconnected building blocks, let me reiterate the point that as you diversify and allocate your assets, you will organize a structure for each of your investments, meaning that you will create entities to hold and manage your investments. This is what the wealthy do. They create businesses to organize the inflow of the multiple streams of revenue that come from diversification and allocation. They then take a portion of the revenue from this asset allocation, put it in a holding account (the corporate name for a Wealth Account), and use that cash as their own bank to invest in and create more diversification and more asset allocation.

Your Money Rules will help you to optimize your investing choices. By following strict criteria on which investments to make, you will move through your selection process on deals much more quickly, take the emotion out of analysis and decision making, and stay focused on meeting short-term objectives and reaching your ultimate vision—your Financial Freedom Day. Though Wealth Cycle Investing is an aggressive, unconventional approach, it is not inherently risky. The opportunities that my team and I seek out are legal, sound, and well within the risk/reward scale. And in this book, I'm showing you how to do what the establishment has always done—take control of your own finances. You do not need a lot of personal experience or even a lot of your own money to get in on these very exciting opportunities. You just need to get a team.

> *Your Money Rules will help you to optimize your investing choices.*

5

Get a Team

Leading Your Wealth

Having a team reduces risk. If you work with others who have experience and knowledge—and possibly even access and funds against which you can leverage your own investment—you increase your upside and reduce your downside. When investing, I have found that collective knowledge and experience lowers risk and accelerates diversification. When you make your way into high-reward investments, you'll find that experience—both your own and that of others—is priceless and an essential ingredient for your success.

Initially, you will pay a price for not having experience. That's the inevitable learning curve. Figuring out how to put together the right team will take time and energy, and maybe money, but it's a necessary part of learning. You lead your wealth by getting a team. This team should consist of trusted

Having a team reduces risk. You lead your wealth by getting a team.

advisors, mentors, professionals, field partners, and utility players who will help you reach your goals. These will be your new best friends. In the Wealth Cycle Investing Worksheet, getting a team is presented as follows:

—TEAM—

LEADER:
FIELD PARTNER:
MENTOR(S):
PROFESSIONALS:
  Entity specialist
  Accountant
  Bookkeeper
  Lawyer
UTILITY PLAYERS:
  Help at work
  Help at home
PARTNERS AND COLLEAGUES:

Leader

The leader of your Wealth Cycle Investing team is *you.* As the leader of your wealth team, it is your responsibility to find every partner on your team, including the experienced people, field partners, mentors, and professionals who will help you to learn and gain experience and knowledge.

This is where it gets a little tricky. Even though you are still learning, you must stay in control of the team and lead your wealth. Two missteps that you can make while building your team are making assumptions about what's happening and abdicating control to others while it's happening. If you make assumptions without asking questions, you miss a chance to learn—and an opportunity to ensure that all those involved are on their game. Assumptions make you less vigilant, and your wealth building needs your attention. Equally, it is never okay to abdicate responsibility, even if you have the best and the brightest at your table. It's difficult not to defer to experts, I know, and I'm not saying that you shouldn't be open to ideas and coachable—you should be exactly that—but you should also always maintain your position as a leader. In Wealth Cycle Investing, you are the leader; you drive your wealth; you are responsible and accountable for everything.

Field Partner

This term is based on a fundamental approach that the wealthy have always used: You must have someone in the industry, in the company, in the town, or on the street (basically someone who is on the inside of the deal or who can get there) helping you to make things happen. The best way to find these people is to ask other people. Say you want to do real estate in Texas. Then you probably want a local broker or property manager as your field partner. To find such a person, you can

- Read the local papers and see what names emerge
- Call the chamber of commerce or local real estate or investment groups and ask some questions to learn who's who
- Find others who have done deals in that area and see who they know
- Try to link yourself to the folks in the inner circles and get the scoop on the local personalities

Once you hear a name pop up a few times, initiate a meeting with this person. Watch her or him in action if you can. You'll see soon enough if this is an appropriate field partner for you. At first, you'll judge these people on their experience and their level of success. You'll then consider their desire. You are looking for a field partner who not only will want to be on the team but will also feel a sense of ownership in the deal. If the field partner is the type of person who likes to have skin in the game and bet on him- or herself, that's good for you, too. Finally, you'll determine if you trust and like this person. Your field partner will be a big part of your business life. It's important that you respect that person. And given the hours you'll put in together, it's important that you also enjoy being with that person. Finding the right field partner in each asset class is essential and is a key component of minimizing risk.

Mentors

Getting experienced people to help you is one of your first steps in investing. Mentors should have a level of experience and success that are beyond your stated goals. In other words, if your goal is a net worth of $1 million, you should talk to someone who has $5 million. In the Jed Stone story, it all began with a phone call. He wanted to learn about the fundamentals, so he called his friend's father, who was a portfolio manager at a bank. Most of my connections to my mentors began in the same way: with a phone call and/or a lunch. A few times I traveled to meet and connect with the mentor in person. Though some people may be unreachable, everyone is worth a try. Remember: someone has already done what you want to do. Don't start from scratch.

If you're feeling insecure about making that call, try to think about what you can offer that person. Maybe it's just pure enthusiasm and energy. Sometimes that's enough. It's important to hold onto those attributes, get over your fear, and realize that you may be doing that person a favor by providing her or him with an opportunity to be a mentor. Employ whatever psychology you need to take action and make that call. Live out loud.

Professionals

At first, your team will consist of those whom you can talk into joining you for a return on the investment or whom you can afford to hire right now. Either way, you'll want to make sure that you always try to get the best people. Mentors are an excellent source of referrals to the right lawyers, accountants, bookkeepers, and other professionals who will help your cause. Without a competent attorney, you will not have airtight contracts and protection. Without a good bookkeeper and tax accountant, you will overpay taxes, thereby limiting your available capital.

Utility Players

Years ago, I realized the *$400 solution.* This is the idea that hiring good help for 10 hours a week at $20 an hour will give you 40 hours of support a month in any area where you need it. Millionaires should not clean their own houses, nor should they mow their own lawns, pay their own bills, deal with their own correspondence, or run their own errands. A millionaire maker's focus is better spent on investments. You want to strengthen your strengths and hire your weaknesses. If you don't have *time,* you need a *team.*

Partners and Colleagues

Every team will have partners and colleagues. These will consist of active and passive investment partners. It will also include strategic partners and colleagues who may or may not be financially involved in the deal but who facilitate the transaction, such as property managers or the management of a business venture.

Obviously teams vary in size and makeup. This list is just a guide and is by no means totally inclusive. Yours, of course, will vary according to each of your deals.

Lead Your Wealth

Leadership and team are two elements that underscore every single step you take in creating and generating your assets. The following are the leadership and team rules you should use as guideposts when following the Wealth Cycle Investing method:

1. **Do not be a lone ranger.** The only way to make millions is through the team-made millionaire approach. For each investment, you must consult your wealth-building mentor and team.
2. **Drive your outcome.** No matter who is on your team, how actively you're involved, or how big or small the deal is, it is you and only you who is in charge of your Millionaire Maker plan. No one will look after or care about your investments as well as you.
3. **Keep it legal.** No contracts, no deal. Period.
4. **Do your homework.** "I don't know" has got to go. You cannot

abdicate control or make assumptions about any aspect of your investing. Your days of "parking and praying" are over.

In wealth building and in business, this last step, doing your home-work, is called due diligence.

6

Due Diligence

Responsibility and Risk

In Wealth Cycle Investing, you are looking to distinguish between real and perceived risk. This is not to say that there isn't real risk in investing; there is. Sometimes, however, the perceived risk can be greater than the real risk. It's important that you apply your education and experience before making a final decision as to the real risk of an opportunity. You do this through due diligence.

The Art of Due Diligence

Determining real risk starts with due diligence. Due diligence is another way of saying that you should research your investments thoroughly through a process of inquiry and investigation. Due diligence is the verification of certain details in any given deal, usually by lawyers, financial analysts, and accountants.

In Wealth Cycle Investing, you do your own direct asset allocation deals, and although some investment specialists may be involved, you remain responsible for your investment decisions. In fact, you should begin to think of yourself as a Wall Street portfolio manager. You are managing a portfolio of diversified assets, and with the help of your team you will assume a fiduciary responsibility—a trusted relationship in which one acts in the best interest of the person whose money or property he or she holds. A key aspect of such responsibility for you and your team is performing due diligence on everything, every time. When the deals get going, you'll engage accountants and lawyers to help you, and there are even professional due diligence firms that can help, but you will do the initial inquiry, continue the research, ask the questions, and kick a lot of tires yourself.

The goal of due diligence is to put yourself in a situation in which you know as much as possible because this knowledge can help you reduce risk.

I think due diligence is one of the most interesting aspects of the investing process. The goal is to put yourself in a situation in which you know as much as possible because this knowledge can help you reduce risk.

Due diligence, which ultimately leads to the valuation of an asset, requires escalating levels of investigation in the following sequence:

1. Data
2. Discussion
3. Discovery
4. Diagnosis
5. Decision

Obviously, the process will get easier as you conduct more of these investigations. The best way to learn how to do due diligence is to have someone on your team who has previously performed due diligence in the particular asset class you're considering. But don't be discouraged if your first attempt at data collection takes months. This learning process will help inform all of your future due diligence.

Data Collection

In order to understand the basics of any asset class or investment opportunity, it helps to do some research. The Internet has opened up a whole new world of investigation for those conducting due diligence, making this first step in the process much easier than it's ever been in the past. A good initial approach is to read as much as you can about the asset in which you're interested. Sources include

- Trade publications
- Local market newspapers
- Industry sector magazines
- Financial newspapers
- Wall Street research reports
- Business magazines
- Investment and finance textbooks
- Investment and finance Web sites and search engines
- DVDs and CDs of experts sharing information about the asset
- Radio talk and news shows
- Television finance and investing programs
- Financial news channels
- Financial and investment newsletters
- Lectures and seminars

- Continuing education classes
- Information from leading experts who *do* deals rather than just talk about doing them

This first stage in the process is nonnegotiable. It's not fair to approach anyone about anything unless you've done some homework. Chances are you will find this phase to be quite enlightening. While you may have thought private equity would be a primary asset of choice for you, you may learn that you don't have the patience or the passion for the kind of study, investigation, and networking that private equity investing requires. It's good to discover these things early on, and this research stage will help you do that.

In addition, each of the asset classes has its own language and culture, filled with acronyms and jargon. That's just the way of the direct-asset investing world and can't be helped; everyone seems to enjoy verbal shortcuts. And, you just can't beat initials to get a point across. In the wealth-building field, the term *ROI* is thrown around like a verbal tic. ROI means return on investment, a term that even when spelled out, can seem a little intimidating to some novice investors. But let's just look at this one term to show you how easy it is to dissect and simplify the language of wealth building.

Return on investment literally means how much you will get (the return) on what you put in (the investment). ROI is always given as a percentage, and it's most often calculated as an annual percentage, although sometimes the total ROI is stated. If you put your money in a bank that gives 3 percent interest, your ROI is 3 percent. If you buy a house for $100,000 and sell it a year later for $150,000, your return on that investment is 50 percent. If you buy a Laundromat for $300,000 and it gives off cash of $30,000 a year for the next 10 years, your annual ROI is 10 percent. If your exit strategy is to sell the

Laundromat at the end of those 10 years and it's appreciated in value to, let's say, $400,000, you'll also enjoy, at the time of the sale, a return on that investment of 33 percent. Overall, your annual ROI for that Laundromat was 13.3 percent. If you put that annual ROI back into the company, instead of taking the cash out every year, then the return is going to compound and your overall ROI will be even greater. There you go, the ABCs of the ROI. Simple. And variations on this theme run throughout the finance field. These include ROA (return on assets), ROE (return on equity), ROS (return on sales), and many more.

None of this is terribly difficult. It's just different. The belief that wealthy people are smart has more to do with perception than with any reality. Some of the most brilliant minds in the world have little in the bank, and I've seen too many average Joes and Janes with millions in assets to think that genius has anything to do with money.

Just as important as finding information is how you absorb it. As you know, there is bias in almost everything you read, including this book and my belief in the Wealth Cycle process. When we're learning, we tend to absorb material unconditionally. In investing and finance, it's important to be aware of this tendency. Because so much of wealth building is based on theory and the wealth builder's own experience, you must evaluate others' opinions carefully. Though there are thousands of wealth builders out there who are currently engaged in their own Wealth Cycle process, there are many people who have realized that our approach was not right for them. That's important. You have to know yourself well enough to recognize whether something resonates or not. Of course, this can be difficult when you're learning, because everything is new and you have few points of reference.

Do your best to cast a critical eye on the information. Read as much as you can, and compare and contrast. What seems right to you will soon surface. Maybe you'll even be lucky enough to have some old beliefs turned upside down, just as long as this comes after some real thinking on your part. I can't tell you the number of times I've seen information on the Internet or even on TV that's misleading—or, worse, just plain wrong. This is where, as with investing, diversification comes in handy. Collect your information from as many sources as possible, and more often than not you'll be closer to being right than to being wrong. Additionally, you should always understand that each book or TV show is written for a specific target audience. If you're listening to an expert on the radio who swears that the floods are coming and that you'd better build an ark, well, you need to make a conscious decision as to whether that's the right expert for you to be listening to. Research the experience and results of team members to be certain they walk their talk.

Courses, lectures, workshops, and seminars are another efficient way to gain a basic knowledge of finance. For some people, a full course might be too much, but there are several continuing education programs that have one-time weekend workshops. I can tell you that, based on the experiences with the one-day Team Made Millionaire seminars and weekend-in-the-streets real estate tours my company runs, people can learn plenty from such intense, bootcamp-esque learning experiences. Show the same vigilance in choosing these courses as you do when choosing your magazines and Web sites. Be picky about the organizations to which you give your time and your ear, not to mention your entrance fee. Ask for recommendations and testimonials from others who have attended the program. Be very wary of get-rich-quick schemes. Money that comes in fast tends to go out even faster.

Data collection is a great way for you to begin leading your wealth. You will feel immediately empowered by taking on this responsibility personally, and your knowledge will increase exponentially. Soon you'll know more than most, but even then this step in the inquiry can never be skipped over. I'm always reading, listening, and looking out for new information.

Discussion

Put the pencil behind your ear, get the pad of paper in hand, and start calling yourself Scoop. It's time to be an asset junkie journalist. True asset addicts, which is what most of the people in the Wealth Cycle become, know how to ask good questions, which means finding people of whom you can ask these questions. To build a list of potential interviews, start with the world you know: mentors, colleagues, and friends who have done similar deals. Your own network is a good place to start because you will feel comfortable asking those people basic questions about the fundamentals of the asset class in which you're interested. These include learning its

- Vocabulary
- Players
- Geography
- History
- Cycles
- Trends
- Qualitative measures
- Quantitative measures

Ask as many questions as you need to, even the seemingly obvious ones. The saying is that there's no such thing as a dumb question, but let's get real; there are indeed dumb questions—and we've all sighed through them. But if you don't know the answer, the question still needs to be asked. I think it takes a lot of courage and intelligence to ask the basic questions. Too many people skip over the obvious for fear of how they'll be perceived. In due diligence, assuming and guessing at anything increases your risk, and that's not the direction we want risk to go. Be smart about those very fundamental questions and ask them of someone you trust, or at least someone who seems nice enough not to condescend to you, or sigh too loudly.

What makes the discussion step in the due diligence process work so well is human nature—people like to talk.

What makes the discussion step in the due diligence process work so well is human nature—people like to talk. Though you may have a ream of questions, sometimes it's best to offer to take the local commercial real estate magnate to lunch, ask him or her a few leading questions, and then just let the magnate reveal all.

Leading questions include

- How did you get started investing in _____?
- What was the best deal you ever did?
- What was the worst mistake you ever made?
- What are the mistakes most people make when looking at _____?
- What are some of the things to look for when you invest in _____?
- Are there others as knowledgeable as you that you can suggest I talk to?

And here's the one that always seems to get the mouths moving:

- What questions should I have asked you that I didn't?

If you think that this person would be a good mentor or colleague for you, you might want to continue the conversation by asking if you can sit in on or tag along on a few meetings or even listen in on some phone calls. You would be surprised how many people are willing to help and how often they'll agree to let you come along. It behooves them to, because they never know where their next deal or investor may be coming from. Again, you must be discerning in finding your mentors; make sure that these people have values that resonate with yours. Honesty, integrity, and fairness are just a few of the values that you will find have staying power in business.

> *Honesty, integrity, and fairness are just a few of the values that you'll find have staying power in business.*

I found one of my first mentors by picking up the phone and cold-calling someone in the field in which I wanted to work. It took a few phone calls, but eventually I got the face-to-face meeting and sowed the seeds of a fertile business relationship. Some of the people who might be able to give you information include

- Advisors of acquaintances or friends
- Local business leaders
- High-net-worth individuals
- Executives in organizations that you admire
- Financial reporters and writers
- Investment bankers
- Corporate and finance lawyers
- Accountants
- Academics

Again, anyone you talk with is going to have a very personal take on the subject at hand, based on her or his own perspective and experience. When you ask, "How much risk is there in gold?" the answer that a wealthy individual gives might be very different from the theories of a professor. Your job is to collect as much reliable information as you have the time and energy for, and then to synthesize that information into ideas that resonate with your needs and objectives.

When you actually get into the discovery portion of due diligence, you are going to widen your search for information. There are times when the more fruitful and insightful conversation is with the factory's machinists, not its executives.

Discovery

Once you've done your research and asked the right questions, you will be up to speed on the generalities of the asset class or even of a specific investment opportunity. The next step is where you dig in deep. It's almost like a field trip or internship, where you open the door, walk in, look around, and kick those tires. Now obviously, some asset classes have no doors to open, but you know, it's a metaphor.

The first step in discovery is to find a checklist of financial, operational, organizational, and sector details that you should know about that asset. Though there are some fundamental questions that cross all asset classes, there are many that are very specific to each. Though you can look at general specifications and measurements, you should have a tailored checklist for each investment that you look into. Compiling and executing these checklists will take some experience, and I highly recommend doing a lot of borrowing. Your mentor, colleagues, lawyers, and accountants in this field probably have a due diligence checklist that you can adapt. Again, as you do this more often and learn from your own mistakes, you will get better at building and creating your own checklist.

Beware of bad information. When you begin, you may not be able to tell the good from the bad, so it always pays to run the information past a mentor and other team members who are helping you. This is also the reason why you want to get in on deals with others that you trust, people who have done it before and have succeeded. These leads may come to you from the discussion stage. But even then, it is still your job to engage in discovery. You are responsible for the risk; you are responsible for the reward; you are accountable for your own decisions. You and only you lead your wealth.

A due diligence checklist can mean many things to many people, but most investors are looking at the same underlying questions that I touched on in the section on discussion. The following is a very general list, which will become more specific and complex when we look at different asset classes.

- The business opportunity, the product, service, property, or concept—in other words, what the asset is offering
- The target market—customer and consumer segments
- Marketing and sales strategies
- Operations
- The industry—market trends, market history, current situation
- The competition—other players, properties, or products in the field
- The supply and demand channels—vendors and retailers (relationships and reliability)
- The management—the executives and professionals, the team
- The organization—employees, locations, partnerships, joint ventures, subsidiaries

- Legal, environmental, tax, and special liabilities issues
- Intangible assets, intellectual property, and goodwill
- The financial analysis: income, balance sheets, cash flow, breakevens, comparables, valuations, and deal structure

Before you get nervous, let me hit that last thing first—math is your friend. Let me assure you, once you start doing numbers, you will not be able to stop. Remember, before you understood multiplication even 2 × 3 was difficult. You can learn anything and everything you need to know about financial analysis, and there are plenty of people around who can help you with the parts you can't figure out yourself. There are millions of people who do this type of analysis every single day, which is proof enough—if millions can do it, so can you.

The best due diligence is conducted when good questions are asked. The best questions usually surface when more than one person is asking those questions. That's why you should gather as many brains as possible for your due diligence. Your team needs knowledge, experience, and creativity in order to ask the best questions and to be successful. Professionals that you should include on your due dili-

The best due diligence is conducted when good questions are asked.

gence team are lawyers, bankers, accountants, property or product specialists, and area or industry experts.

The following summary will give you direction on how to go about asking the best questions. These are the questions I ask when surveying an asset, and they represent my bias based on my experiences.

Understand the Opportunity

First and foremost, I like to understand the assets I'm considering. I want to know what the asset is and what it does. What's the offering?

In other words, what's the product, the service, or, in the case of real estate, the property? I also like to understand what's distinct about this product, property, service, or concept, its strategy, and its positioning in the market. I like to see a singular and sustainable competitive advantage, which may come in the form of the product or service itself or in the way in which it is offered and delivered to the market. Brand equity could be crucial for products and services in certain categories, and so sometimes I look for that. The size of the company offering the product or the size of the property is also important because I like to see that the business or property has the capacity to support its strategy and deliver on its promise. Sometimes, as in certain real estate deals, I don't want the property to be too big if I'm not sure that the demand will match the supply. I may also like an asset that's innovative, because it will shake up a current paradigm, or maybe in some cases I'll fear that the asset is too innovative and won't be accepted or supported.

Know Your Target Markets

I like to know to whom the asset is going to appeal—in other words, where my cash will be coming from. Sometimes this is a customer like a wholesaler or a retailer, and sometimes it's the consumer, like the guy eating in the restaurant or the tenant of the building. An attractive investment opportunity is a concept, company, or property that has captured a very specific segment of a market, created significant barriers to entry for its competitors, and still has the potential for growth. In these cases, I am careful to consider whether the asset is just a novelty, or whether it has real staying power with its users or renters. In technology, this happens all the time, and in real estate, this can be the difference between

Look for assets that are insulated from competition and have a sustainable, enduring attribute.

a boom and a bust market. The loyalty and stickiness of the target market is also important, because if the product, service, property, or concept can be easily duplicated, then competitors can easily undermine the value of your asset. I'm always looking for an asset that might be insulated from competition and has some sustainable, enduring attribute that will continue to capture a specific segment of customers or consumers.

Marketing and Sales

These strategies and the team are important for any asset. Making a product or building a property or creating a new technology or providing a clever service is worthwhile only if it's what the market wants and can get. If I'm investing in a private company or a technology or a raw material, I want to understand how the marketing mix—that is, the product, price, place, and promotion—is derived. This includes the benefits or promise of the business, property, product, or service; its pricing strategy; the distribution channels used to get the product to market or where the property is located; and the promotion used to position the offering in the marketplace. All of these are key to the venture's success. Additionally, I want to see a sales force and a strategy that can complete the transaction that marketing has set up. It's one thing to bring them in the door; it's another to seal the deal. Many times in my private business venture due diligence I find that this ability is lacking, which means there is an opportunity for profitable growth.

Operations

The product or property may be beautiful on the surface, but if it's not structurally sound on the inside, then it might not be for me. On the other hand, if an investor can bring ideas for operational efficiencies to the asset, he or she can get in on the asset at a discount

and immediately improve its value. This
is true for the restoration and renovation
of any real estate property. Operations
covers every aspect of how an asset is

> **Operations lies at the heart of any asset.**

put together, processed, built, or excavated; it lies at the heart of
any asset.

Understand the Industry

No asset is an island. Its value can ebb and flow with the industry's
fortunes. If a residential property is the first one available in an area
where there's been an influx of residents, then demand for that property could be solid. If the market is saturated because the rest of the
industry has already built there, I don't want to buy into yet another
property that's going up. Industry *trends* are an essential component
of evaluating the asset. If the asset is a private company that makes
sneakers, but the industry trends show a movement toward clogs,
then I've got to reconsider my choice. The *history* of a certain industry is also very important and too often overlooked. Concepts tend
to come and go in cycles, and it's rare that an idea hasn't popped up
before. I've seen assets that boast a distinct, innovative advantage,
only to discover that the same idea surfaced and failed 30 years ago.

The Competition

An asset is usually valued based on how it compares to other similar assets. In fact, one of the valuation methods used by Wall Street
is called *comparables*. This means that the analyst ascribes a value
to an asset based on how that asset's attributes and benefits compare to those of a set of similar assets. Understanding the what,
who, and where of the other assets in the category is essential to
understanding both the perceived and the real value of your investment.

Supply and Demand Relationships

Every asset depends on other assets in a vertical chain that gets it to its final end user. If the source of raw materials is not reliable, or if the owner of the transportation on which the asset relies for its components has a reputation for being antagonistic, or if the retailer or broker through which the asset gets to market holds all the cards, then these things can have a huge effect on the viability of an asset and undermine its growth.

No asset is an island.

The Management

There are many individuals, and I'm one of them, who invest in people, not things. I've seen the best ideas in the world go down the drain because their champions had no character, and I've seen the craziest ideas make it to the top based solely on the excellent leadership skills of management. Wall Street values management so much that the stocks of public companies will often trade at a premium solely because they have great CEOs. The person behind your investment and that individual's history in the asset class always need to be an area of inquiry.

The Organization

You can tell a lot about an asset from its people. Employees whose work is directly involved and the strategic relationships and key partners who have an impact say a lot about an asset and are vital links to understanding the investment. How the asset is organized is important, too. If a solar energy company has its headquarters in Seattle and its branches in the Amazon rainforest, there might be a disconnect going on. In real estate, if I don't think the management has hired good property managers to oversee the asset, I might not give it a second look.

Legal, Environmental, Tax, and Other Liabilities

There are many issues that can pop up in an asset that you might not even know to look for. Old litigation might be pending, ready to take all the value out of the asset. That 70 acres of land in Tennessee that looked perfect for a preconstruction play might have an Environmental Protection Agency issue that the owner hasn't discovered yet. Net operating loss carryforwards prevent earnings from being fully taxed and thus create the perception of higher earnings. Underfunded pension plans can be a huge liability. For any asset, it's a good idea to pick up the rocks and see what crawls out. Lawyers, environmental specialists, tax attorneys, and accountants can be very helpful in looking at these items.

Intangible Assets, Intellectual Property, and Goodwill

Many assets derive a lot of their value from that ethereal intangible called "intellectual property." These are usually ideas or perceptions tied to the business that have more of a conceptual value. This is especially true of assets with huge brand awareness and technology companies that rely on innovation. It can also be true of glamorous real estate properties, like a ski lodge or a shopping mall. You will pay a premium for these intangibles, so you should be sure that they are worth it.

The Financials

Your *real* financials are your revenue and expenses, assets, and liabilities. We modeled these on the income statements and balance sheets of companies. When you're looking at an asset—any asset—the financials are the nuts and bolts. I know some real estate asset addicts who won't even visit a property until they've looked over the financials once, twice, or several times. This is usually the first step in discovery, because no one who knows anything about due diligence is going to waste his or her time with any of the rest of it unless the numbers match his or her requirements and objectives. I like to think of financials as the mirror that doesn't lie. That doesn't mean, however, that they don't fib a little here and there. That's why the rest of the discovery process is imperative. We'll go over the financials in more depth in the next chapter, on valuation.

Knowing the questions, from the data and discussion steps, and getting the answers, in the discovery phase, will include an up-close and personal inspection of the asset and its management.

Diagnosis and Decision

In the diagnosis stage, you assemble all of your facts and figures and match them against your Money Rules. Have your team review them as well; more eyes on the project provides greater perspective. If the asset is sound and meets your criteria for investing, then you might see this as a good opportunity for your portfolio. Diagnosis is not simple. You, with help from your team, must decide if this is or is not a healthy asset. That determination simplifies the decision to invest or not to invest.

Due Diligence in Action

Once you've gathered your data, had your discussions with preliminary contacts, prepared and completed your discovery, made a diagnosis, and delivered your decision, you've completed your due diligence. This level of due diligence on each and every asset might seem a bit tedious and intricate. And it is. Due diligence is different for every asset. What's important is that you understand the spirit of due diligence and use the sequence and the questions to take responsibility for your investment by reducing your risk through knowledge.

The sooner you start, the sooner you will create the can-do equation that gets you from action to confidence. I'm an asset addict for no reason other than that I like it. Once I got started, I was in. I think you'll discover that managing your own wealth makes you feel more secure, in control, and responsible. It also is tremendously satisfying, in and of itself and in terms of the community of people who start to gather around to invest together.

I've made investments with a very quick due diligence process that went something like this: (1) Look at the numbers carefully, (2) call the management team and talk to the key players, (3) run some numbers on other properties or products established as a comparable group for the asset, (4) visit the business, and finally (5) make a diagnosis and a decision. I've sometimes completed this whole process in one day's work. When that happens, it's usually because I have a lot of experience with that asset class or have intimate knowledge of the particular asset.

Picking a Market . . . from the Street

Let's look at the due diligence process in action. The process applies to any type of investment, but let's use buying cash-flow houses as an example of picking a market. Remember, your job is to lead your due diligence, not necessarily to do it all.

Data

One of the first decisions in cash-flow real estate investing is to determine the market or markets you want to invest in. Look for markets where prices are relatively low and rents are relatively high compared to other markets. This ratio of average rent divided by average price is a good way to quickly narrow down the list of potential markets. Once you have a shorter list of markets, see if the rents are high enough to pay for all costs of owning the house yet leave some cash flow each month.

Also look for markets (and submarkets within markets) that are expecting job growth or other trends that point toward a greater need for housing. Who are the major employers, and are they growing or cutting back their operations? Is there an influx of new residents and businesses? The smart investor gets an idea of what data is needed and starts the research on the Internet.

Other potential data sources for real estate investing include the U.S. Census, well-known real estate Web sites like realtor.com and domania.com, magazine articles, economic development agencies, and the many Web sites of active players in local markets. Knowing what you're looking for and persistence in searching are key to gathering the data you will need.

Discussion

Ask your team members if they have any experience in investing in cash-flow houses or in the local real estate markets that interest you. Leverage their knowledge to help you refine the questions you want answered and where that data might be found. I always ask my team to refer me to other people and resources to help in the analysis.

I often hear back from my community of wealth builders that they almost always end up digging deeper because of what they learn along the way. But beware, some investors get trapped in the endless loop of gathering data and never get to taking any meaningful action; we call this "analysis paralysis." Your job is to know just enough to make an informed, intelligent decision and to assess the risk factors.

Let's assume you have an idea of the types of properties you want and have learned enough to pick your first target market. At this point, you should have a very short list of markets of interest. Now speak with experts in these local markets, including property managers, Realtors who specialize in serving investors, and other investors who find deals in which to participate.

Once you identify good-looking deals, find local experts or field partners to join your team. If it sounds like there are cash-flow deals available, share your specific criteria and get their perspective on whether your needs can be met in their market. Screen your team carefully. Narrow it down to those who know their market the best and can help you the most.

Discovery

Discovery is when direct action begins. This is when to make your agenda for a market visit, schedule appointments, and make it happen. This includes meeting with your field partners in the local market, driving through potential submarkets, looking at several properties, and asking lots of questions. Think of yourself as a combination of explorer and detective looking for evidence that leads you to great investments. It's important to leave any personal housing expectations at home. You are looking for houses that will make you money, not for a place to live.

Your explorer side uses your powers of observation, communication, and intuition to gather as much detailed information as possible. Your intuition also plays a role, especially as you consider your field partners. Do you intuitively trust or not trust them? Do they seem to know what they are talking about? Push the potential field partners for their opinions on specific investments and the reasons for those opinions.

Diagnosis

After working the market through the discovery phase, you can draw your own informed conclusions about the market and its investment potential. But beyond your own assessment, whom on your team have you involved in reviewing the market and any potential deals? Whether it's a specialist on research or in assessing the deal, or a mastermind team member or fellow investor reviewing your work and conclusions, outside input is critical in broadening your perspective.

The last part of diagnosis is confirming how, specifically, you'll fit this investment opportunity into your overall portfolio and wealth plan. Said another way, double-check your plan for a new cash flow market and make adjustments based on what you learned from researching the market. What are your final criteria for cash-flow house investing in a new market? Did they change from your criteria before researching the market, and if so, what's different and why? How will you measure your results and get feedback to improve them? How much cash and credit are you now targeting toward your new market? How many houses do you plan to buy, and when? Who made the cut and will join your local team? What roles do you need to play in leading this team?

Think of this last part as something analogous to a pilot doing a preflight checklist to minimize the risk of something going wrong during the flight. It's rare to find a problem, but you want to find it on the ground, not in the air.

Decision

This decision is not an emotional one but rather a logical and obvious one; it comes from knowing your objectives and having done the due diligence on whether the market meets your investing goals.

Direct and Accessible Assets

Learning the business of the due diligence trade may be unfamiliar but it is not difficult when you are a part of a team. Because most of the deals done in Wealth Cycle Investing are private deals, they require a fair amount of due diligence. In the following chapters, we're going to look at a few deals and how to conduct the evaluation that gets you to a yes or no decision, but for now, let's take a look at a manufacturing and distribution company that caught my eye. This company made private-label nutritional products, and its owners wanted to initiate their exit strategy.

Data

With most private ventures, there is very little publicly accessible information. That is, of course, one of the advantages of being privately held and one of the challenges for companies that are going public. That is not to say that sources are limited. First and foremost, the owners of this company were looking to sell, so I did not have to go sneaking around the back door of the factory and then come in with some Heigh-Ho Silver hostile offer. They had already created a private placement memorandum (PPM), which is an overview of the business that provides a substantial amount of information on the concept offering, the management, the organization, and the financials. Each PPM usually includes the deal structure, and it is very important to recognize that the structure of each deal is different. The team that puts the PPM together may have ways of creating what it thinks is a fair deal, but this may not be what you or your lawyer considers fair. You want to be in deals where you actually make money if the company makes money and you are not liable if it does not. Believe me, some deals are structured so that this is not the case, so be careful.

The PPM almost always starts with something like this: "An investment in a company such as this involves a high degree of risk." In other words, it's got a nice beat, but you can't dance to it unless you are an accredited investor. If you want to get into this game, OPM and OPC (other people's credit or credentials) and a team are a great way to do this.

This deal came to me from one of my field partners who was leading the effort. He had helped to create the preliminary documents that led to the PPM, and I trusted that he'd done a lot of the due diligence ahead of me, which meant that I knew that I was duplicating his efforts and watching his back—this helped us both.

In addition to the PPM, other sources of information that I scoured included the industry trade magazines. These publications are helpful in understanding the arena and competition. I also fleshed out a list of what I thought were close to comparable companies, including some publicly traded ones, to give me some perspective on the company, its operations, and its market.

Discussion

I immediately began looking for people who had experience with the industry, though I wasn't specific about the particular asset at this time because I feared a bidding war. My team of mentors and professionals helped me to find other experienced investors and professionals who understood this asset class. I then spoke to customers, who consisted of some large retail chains and the end consumers who actually used the asset's products. After this, I felt ready to call management directly and ask my favorite conversation starter, "Why are you selling this business?" Sometimes it's the *way* they answer

> *Due diligence is about translating perceived risk into real risk by fully understanding the opportunity at hand.*

this, not *what* they say, that's most interesting. If I hear a flinch in the speaker's voice, or see eyes cast down and shuffling feet, my confidence in the asset is going to fade.

Discovery

Because my field partner had established himself with the management, and I had presented myself as a serious and interested investor who could add value to the venture, the door opened wide. I really enjoy this aspect of due diligence: walking around the plant and machines, watching the flow of operations—it's satisfying. I look for the inefficiency, where there is a gap that, when filled, will create substantial profits.

Diagnosis

It was the financials and marketing strategy that made the strongest impression as I went about my due diligence effort. This company was flush with cash flow, and I like cash flow. It also had a lot of growth potential because the marketing strategy had been very narrow and restrained, focusing on only a few channels of distribution. Additionally, I was very impressed with the company's scientists, who were coming up with new product ideas every day, and the company's strategy for idea flow coming from demand was appealing.

Decision

We decided yes. My field partner and I put a team together and did the deal. That was, and continues to be, a smart move.

I realize that although this deal was less accessible than a publicly traded company's stock, it was more accessible to me than it was to the average investor. But that's only because the average investor tends to play a little game. Though I started out on the perimeter of the outside circle, I have been focusing on bigger deals for years now, and I continue to find my way into bigger and better opportunities. This will happen to you, too. It's an inevitable benefit of accelerating the Wealth Cycle.

Due diligence is about translating perceived risk into real risk by fully understanding the opportunity at hand. How much that opportunity is worth, its value, and where that value is headed is the *valuation* piece of the equation.

7

Valuation

Show Me the Money

A a term that investors use for determining the value of an asset is *valuation*. It's one thing to look at an asset and to understand the concepts behind it and the demand for it, but it's quite another to understand its intrinsic value. It almost goes without saying that valuation is the cornerstone of investing. When we talk about value, we're talking about three things:

1. Present value
2. Current perceived value
3. Future value

Valuation is the cornerstone of investing.

These values are based on a variety and range of potential influences, and many times they depend on the eye of the beholder. For any asset, such as a real estate property that's on the market, a stock, or a retail chain store, the sellers suggest one value, and the buyers suggest another. This goes on every single second in the stock market, where traders negotiate the "bid" (what the buyer will pay) and the "ask" (what the seller will take) prices back and forth until they can settle. Rarely does anyone's pure valuation of an asset directly match someone else's.

Usually, though, the buyer sees something in the value of the asset that the seller doesn't, and that something—call it potential, perhaps—is the genesis of most transactions. No asset has any value unless it can be converted into currency, and so the annual cash flow or income is one template used to set valuation. The other is the exit strategy. Your exit strategy—how you'll sell the asset—should be part of your plan before you create or acquire an appreciating asset. If your asset creates income for only a limited period of time, as an oil well does, then your exit strategy depends on if and when in the income cycle you sell the asset.

This chapter reviews the structure of basic quantitative valuation, beginning with an overview of some valuation methods, and then a breakdown of financial statements. Then it examines the ways investors use the numbers from these financial statements to analyze assets and determine value. The following primer presents a straightforward introduction to valuation.

Valuing Assets

Valuation is both objective and subjective. The objective factors that contribute to the value of an asset are usually the quantitative attributes, represented by numbers and facts. Subjective factors are qualitative, representing the investor's perception of the asset. For example, an investor who sees great potential in an asset is obviously relying on his or her subjective opinion, as well as on the objective analysis. There are several basic methods for valuing assets, and each asset class has its own metrics, both quantitative and qualitative. In real estate, for example, you can look at comparative sales, cash-on-cash return, and capitalization rates, to name a few of the possibly interesting numbers. On the qualitative side, location and signs of economic growth can create the perception of that asset. In valuing public companies, the

> **Valuation is both objective and subjective.**

price/earnings ratio, and how it compares to those of other companies in the same sector, might be one of the first numbers to catch your eye. On the qualitative side, a lot of emphasis should be put on good management and the target market. In looking at a private company, it is always important to inquire about its book value and how much of its business is financed by its accounts payable. The investor's subjective perception is usually informed by management, any potential for operating efficiencies, what may be seen as possible market trends, and the range of possible marketing strategies.

Obviously, there are a lot of factors to consider. Chapter 6, on due diligence, covers several qualitative attributes of an asset. These qualitative factors have a big influence on how to value an asset:

- The concept or product offering
- The strategies and operations
- The market
- The management team

In a concept or product offering, look for a distinct advantage or a new idea that meets a real market need. In strategies, it is important to see efficiency and effectiveness, in addition to a well-thought-out model for how the revenue will continue to come into the asset. In the market, look for demand, as well as the capacity for customers and consumers to accept the concept. If the distribution channels don't have the tools or the capacity to get that new concept from the maker to the user, then no matter how brilliant the concept is, there's no market for it—and that's not good value. In management, experience and smarts are great assets. The leaders of the asset should have spent considerable time in their industry or with that asset in particular, and they should have the expertise to execute innovative, competitive, sustainable, and profitable strategies while adapting to the changes in their environment. Investments are often made by good leaders with a vision and with the character and capacity to carry off that vision. Ownership structure is also important, especially in publicly traded companies where large blocks are owned by families or companies that may significantly affect business strategy.

Sometimes the qualitative factors can draw you into an asset. Other times, the numbers prevail. Many of the qualitative aspects of an investment are uncovered during due diligence. The purpose of this chapter is to get you started on the numbers—the objective analysis.

For some of you, numbers make your head spin. They have that effect on almost everyone at first—more evidence of the exclusive jargon that keeps the uninitiated out of the club. The important thing to recognize is that although the numbers may appear endless, there are only a limited number of quantitative criteria by which to measure assets. As you start to do more research on the assets in which you are interested, you'll encounter a lot of repetition, and soon enough the numbers will sink in.

But if your head starts to spin too much as you read this chapter, just skim through it. You do not need to absorb all of this fully today. My objective is to introduce you to the language of quantitative valuation. As with learning any language, it takes usage and action to really get it. The goal is to give you a foundation from which to start growing.

There are a lot of people who do valuation, who enjoy it, and who do it well. They will join your team as you build it. Even though I am very comfortable with and even enjoy numbers, I have valuation specialists on my teams. It's a happy day, by the way, when you find a good quant jock for your team. I highly recommend it. Wealth Cycle Investing does require that you lead your wealth, however, so you need to have some understanding of what's going on in those spreadsheets.

> *To lead your wealth, you need to have some understanding of what's going on in those spreadsheets.*

Quantitative Value: Financial Statements

One thing that you'll find helpful in learning about asset valuation is that the numbers used to derive value come from only three financial statements. These three statements are universal approaches to presenting the value of a company or investment.

1. **The income statement.** The income statement, sometimes called the profit and loss (P&L) statement, is a monthly, quarterly, or annual snapshot of revenues and expenses and the resulting profit or loss during that period of time.
2. **The balance sheet.** The balance sheet tells what assets the business has at a particular date, how much is owed on those assets (debt or liabilities), and how much of them are owned (the equity).
3. **The cash-flow statement.** The cash-flow statement shows how the real cash, not just the numbers used for accounting purposes, goes into and out of the business.

These three statements tell the financial story of an asset. If we're looking at historical performance, they will contain actual data. On the other hand, we can use the same formats to project future performance. These are called *pro forma* statements and contain our best guess at what performance may happen in the future time period.

The data in these statements allow us to do some analyses to determine the current or future value of a potential investment. For example, a breakeven analysis is often used for start-ups; it shows the amount of sales needed if the company is to break even after all expenses. A net present value, sometimes called discounted cash flow analysis, is used for evaluating acquisitions and capital investments. There are many more financial analyses, each of them a specific tool for a specific purpose. Now, if you're looking at real estate, or commodities like gold, these statements are going to look different from the financials of a consumer products company, but the fundamentals are the same.

All these financial statements will be covered in this chapter. We will then look at types of quantitative and qualitative analysis that you might find helpful for several different assets. All of this information can be found in any basic accounting book, and there are also some easy-to-use workbooks for entry-level high school and college classes. You might want to take a few hours to read some of these. Doing so will help you become comfortable with the concepts. The following is a very basic and surely incomplete rundown to give you a big-picture view of the sources of asset valuation.

The Income Statement, or P&L

The income statement provides a summary of income and expenses, usually done on a monthly, quarterly, and annual basis. The purpose of an income statement is to determine profitability. Basically an income statement looks like this:

REVENUE (HOW MUCH MONEY COMES IN THROUGH SALES)
− COST OF GOODS SOLD (COGS; EXPENSES DIRECTLY RELATED TO MAKING THE PRODUCT)
= GROSS PROFIT (GP; REVENUE − COGS)
= SGA (SALES, GENERAL, ADMINISTRATIVE, OVERHEAD, OR OPERATING EXPENSES)
= OPERATING PROFIT, SOMETIMES CALLED EBIT*, (GP − SGA)
− INTEREST (INTEREST ON DEBT IS TAX DEDUCTIBLE)
− TAXES (WHAT YOU OWE THE GOVERNMENT)
= NET INCOME
*EARNINGS BEFORE INTEREST AND TAXES

The income statement is always vertical, which is important because its visual appearance has become part of the financial vocabulary. For example, "the bottom line" is often used to mean net income. Additionally, "above the line" and "top of the line" items usually refer to certain items in revenues, and "below the line" refers to items in operating expenses. And so on. Many words in income statements are used interchangeably. For example, some people say gross profit, while others call it gross income. Sales, general, administrative (SGA) expenses are also called overhead or operating expenses. Don't blink; this happens a lot. That should actually give you some confidence in learning these concepts.

We get a lot of valuation metrics from the income statement. Often income statement items are represented as percentages of sales, or margins. Everyone looking at investments loves to talk about margins, and this is a very straightforward concept. For example, let's say that revenues are $200 and the cost of goods sold (COGS) is $80; then the gross profit (GP) is $120 and the gross profit margin, or gross margin, is the percentage that $120 is of $200, or 60 percent.

Over time, you'll notice that within each industry or asset class, there tend to be standard margins. When you are considering a food company, for example, you might be looking for and expecting lower gross margins than if you were looking at a clothing company, where the COGS tends to be less than that for food companies.

These comparable industry metrics are everything in valuation. Any company or property that experiences lower margins than its competitors always has some explaining to do. Value investors seek margins that are lower than those of the comparables because they want to see if there is an opportunity to pay less for the asset now and enjoy some profitability just by increasing the margins.

The Balance Sheet

The balance sheet lies at the heart of valuation because it reveals the investment's makeup. The balance sheet is an x-ray, a document split right down the middle that shows what is owned (the investment's assets) on the left, and what is owed (debt) and who owns it (equity) on the right. The total of assets and the total of debt plus equity are always equal. That's where the statement gets its name—the right side and the left side of the statement always balance.

$$Assets = Liabilities\ (Debt + Equity)$$

Assets
The assets are listed on the left side of the balance sheet. Assets are always listed in order of liquidity. Liquidity is how fast or easily an

asset can be turned into cash. Obviously, the most liquid asset you can have is cash. Some assets, like stocks and bonds, can be sold quickly for cash and so are very liquid. Other assets, like heavy equipment and factories, take a long time to sell. These are considered less liquid. They are classified as long-term assets and are shown toward the bottom of the assets column. Intangible assets, or intellectual property and goodwill, discussed previously, are at the bottom of the assets column. These assets are not traditionally liquid. People who license intellectual property are very good at turning these assets into cash, but these items are still listed at the bottom of the column.

Liabilities

Liabilities, or debt and equity are listed on the right side of the balance sheet. These are in order of obligation. The most senior obligations are those that must be paid back first.

Debt

Debt is the first thing in the liability section of the balance sheet. Debt holders receive interest payments and get their money back on a specified date, so this is an obligation of the company. Debt is classified as short term or long term, based on when these loans are due. Short-term liabilities, or those that must be paid back within a year, are listed first.

Equity

Owner's equity is at the bottom of the right side of the balance sheet. Equity represents the investments of shareholders. Since this is ownership, there is no obligation to pay it back. The investors are betting that they will receive a higher return on their investment than the debt holders are getting. This return would come through growth and potential income of the business or property.

This is the basic rundown, but balance sheets look different depending on the industry. Take a commercial bank, for instance.

Assets	*Liabilities*
Cash	Debt
Accounts receivable	Accounts payable
Stocks and securities	Short-term liabilities
Raw materials	Notes that are due in less than one year
Inventory	Long-term (due after one year) liabilities
Capital equipment	Senior, or bank, debt, at a rate around prime
Plants/buildings	
Intangibles and intellectual property	Mezzanine debt: prime + some percentage more
	Subordinated debt: with a higher rate of interest
	Shareholders Equity
Total Assets = X	Total Liabilities = X

The money that it loans out to clients would seem to be a liability, but it's actually an asset because the bank is making money on that money. The money that a bank has in its safe, kept for its clients, is actually a liability because the bank owes the money to its customers. Once you understand the general concept of a balance sheet, though, it will make sense.

Understanding the balance sheet goes a long way toward understanding financial instruments, specifically debt and equity. Companies need capital (money), and they can get this capital in one of two ways. (In fact, there are variations on these two ways, such as hybrids of both called, "convertibles," but we're not going to touch on those.) Basically, there's debt and there's equity, and these are the items that appear on the right side of the balance sheet. With debt, a company borrows money and pays it back to the investor with interest. Sometimes this debt is called "notes" or "bonds." In real estate, it's called a "mortgage." With equity, the investor buys a piece of the company—that is, a part ownership—in the form of shares or stock.

This need for capital is represented in the public and private markets by stocks and bonds. By taking the time to review and understand the financials, you can see what those stocks and bonds represent. It's all connected.

Cash-Flow Statements

The cash-flow statement and the income statement, discussed earlier in this chapter, are two different things. The cash-flow statement is a dynamic record of the sources of cash and the uses of that cash, with a running tally recorded in a daily, weekly, monthly or annual time frame. The cash-flow statement is quite similar to the P&L; in fact, many people confuse the two at first glance. But the big difference is that the cash-flow statement lists actual expenditures, whereas the P&L lists expenses as defined by the accountants. Again, that means that the P&L may deduct something like the depreciation or amortization of an asset, because it's an expense, but no such entry appears on a cash-flow statement because it's not an actual cash expenditure. However, the asset being depreciated did appear on the cash-flow statement when it was purchased.

I've seen many cash-flow statements in my day, and they tend not to be as standard as the income statement and balance sheet. They are similar to the income statement in that they usually run vertically, starting with the money that comes in, the *sources of cash,* and continuing down to the money going out, the *uses of cash.* For most startups, the statements are done monthly, although many times they are done weekly, and I've even seen them done daily. At first cash flow is usually negative at the bottom of the page. Eventually, the tide turns, and annual cash-flow statements for most investments show positive cash flow. A typical cash-flow statement would look like this:

Cash on Hand—Beginning of Period		
Sources of Cash:		
Cash sales		
Cash from accounts receivable receipts		
Loans and equity taken in		
Interest income		
Total Sources of Cash:		
Uses of Cash:		
Purchases (specify)		
Gross wages (exact withdrawal)		
Payroll expenses (taxes, etc.)		
Outside services		
Supplies (office and operations)		
Repairs and maintenance		
Advertising		
Car, delivery, and travel		
Accounting and legal		
Rent		
Telephone		
Utilities		
Insurance		
Taxes (real estate, etc.)		
Interest		
Other expenses (specify)		
Miscellaneous		
Subtotal		
Loan principal payments		
Capital purchases (specify)		
Other start-up costs		
Reserve and/or escrow		
Owners' withdrawal		
Total Uses of Cash:		
Cash on Hand—End of Period:		

This list is incomplete and suggests only a few sample items. But as you can see just from these few examples, the details tend to be much more specific in the sources and uses statement than they are in the income statement. Instead of just listing overhead expense, for example, there tend to be specific line items for utilities, telephone, office supplies, and so on. The cash-flow statement is an actual accounting of cash going in and out, and as a result, it's detailed.

The initial cash used to create a business is often shown in a cash-flow statement in a column called Capital Development. These numbers are usually very big, and, of course, are mostly uses of cash. As a result, the cash-flow statements of most start-ups show negative cash flow.

For many businesses, cash flow is a better indicator of, and basis for, valuation than profits. Usually, these are capital-intensive businesses, such as telephone companies with cell towers; media conglomerates that own television stations; transportation businesses that own airplanes and trains; real estate organizations with income-generating properties; energy businesses, such as the ones that own oil wells; construction companies and farms with heavy machinery; and retailers that own their own stores. These types of companies are often valued on multiples of cash flow, not earnings.

As you might have noticed in the income statement, operating earnings are often called EBIT (and this, by the way, is pronounced as a word [ē · bit], not as letters). This means earnings before interest and taxes, and it is an important number because it represents the true operating profit, which is the number that wealth builders should care about most. When you are doing a valuation, net income is not that helpful, because the interest number depends on how the company is financed, and the tax number depends on how the entity is structured, as well as on other factors, such as certain expenditures. For each buyer of the asset, the interest and tax numbers will fluctuate, so in order to really look at the value, most wealth builders focus on EBIT.

For capital-intensive companies, where there is a lot of depreciation—an expense, as we discussed, that is purely a paper deduction each year, with no real cash actually going out the door—the EBIT number becomes EBITD, pronounced "ēbit-d," which is earnings before deducting interest, income taxes, and depreciation. That is, you take the earnings and add back interest, taxes, and depreciation. Most folks and industries go one step further and look at EBITDA, which is earnings before (taking out) interest, taxes, depreciation, and amortization. A phrase that you will often hear out of the mouths of the people on Wall Street is, "What's the multiple of EBITDA?" Now you know that they are asking nothing more than "how many times (what's the multiple of) cash flow?"

Valuations are usually based on multiples. That is, how many times (multiples just means multiplication) a certain line item—such as revenue, earnings, EBITDA, or cash flow—is someone willing to pay for that asset? In most asset classes, there are industry norms. For example, an investor might pay 10 times earnings (or a multiple of 10) for an aluminum company but would pay 30 times earnings for a technology company. These multiples reflect the level and speed of growth that's expected. In some industries, the accounting for expenses can be a little subjective, and so investors look only at multiples of sales. In any capital-intensive company, investors look at multiples of cash flow.

The Analyses

As I mentioned, these statements provide a picture of what's happening in a business or a property or any investment opportunity.

We then use the data in these statements to conduct analyses that will help us determine the investment's value.

Breakeven Analysis

Breakeven analysis tells start-up companies how much money they need to take in while paying the running costs of doing business in order to literally break even. Breakeven is the point where the amount the company takes in and pays out is even, so it isn't making money, but it isn't losing money either. The intention of a breakeven analysis is to show investors how long they'll need to wait until the company stops losing money. "*When* is breakeven?" is more often the question than "*What* is breakeven?" What is of interest about the sales and expenses is how they grow in relation to each other and in what time period the sales growth is projected to exceed the expenses.

Net Present Value or Discounted Cash-Flow Analysis

The net present value (NPV) or discounted cash-flow analysis provides a measurement of time, money, and comparable choices in order to judge the quality of an investment. This can be a very simple equation or a big, complicated spreadsheet. The gist of the net present value calculation, though, is that you are looking for today's value, the present value of an asset, so that you can decide how much to pay or take, today, for that asset.

In order to find the present value, you have to estimate how much profit or cash flow the company is going to create every year, over a certain number of years, and then what the future value of that money will be. One standard for measuring how well an investment will or will not do is the very straightforward question, "If I put this cash in the bank, would it make more or less than it would make here in this asset?" By comparing these uses of cash, investors can decide where best to use their money.

You might find it worth your while to look at a few of these equations and have a mentor or advisor walk you through the calculations. The formulas for present value are already built into many spreadsheet programs, and you might find it helpful to investigate these as well.

Numbers and Ratios in the Analysis

What follows is an introduction to the language of valuation, including discussion of some basic valuation measurements for a variety of assets. This should be helpful when you're faking your way through a cocktail party and working your way up to asking mentors the smarter "naïve" questions.

Traditionally, investors consider an asset's income or appreciation potential to be its essential component of value. And you should, too. This is what it's all about: creating cash flow or net worth to build your Wealth Cycle. The rest of the valuation puzzle is about coming up with these two numbers—future earnings (cash flow) and future price (net worth). Really, that's it, that's the core of your world, right there: future earnings or cash flow and future price or value.

The core of your world is future earnings and future price or value.

The Numbers

In order to estimate going forward what these numbers might be(their potential), investors look at several qualitative factors, such as concept, strategy, operations, market, and management, to help them see if the projected quantitative factors can be real. If these qualitative factors look strong, I factor them into the valuation. Then I move on to the following basic numbers:

- Increasing sales
- Steady cash flow or solid earnings growth
- Price/earnings multiples
- Return on investment (ROI)
- Book value

Increasing *sales* are a good indication of a healthy asset. It's basic economics: if demand is increasing, supply will benefit. A way to increase sales is *market share.* If the demand for energy is going up, that's good. If oil and gas is claiming, and will continue to claim, a larger share of that demand than other energy sources, this is a very good sign of future growth. An investor also likes to see *gross profit* and *operating profits,* and their *margins,* increase along with increasing sales. This is imperative, and a look at the income statement shows you that this sliding scale, so to speak, is obvious. If sales go up and gross profit stays flat, then cost of goods sold is getting too high, making the increase in sales futile. If the gross profit goes up in line with the sales, that means the margins are going to be flat, and that's not great either. As the volume of units sold or dollars increases, you want to see efficiencies in gross profits and thus increasing margins, if only by a tad. As we discussed when looking at the income statement, it can also be very telling for valuation to compare an asset's margins to the margins of its comparables. Margins are key to valuation. If, for example, profit margins are already high on an industry's scale, there is less opportunity for gain for the investor.

In a start-up company or an asset that's not yet ready for market, like oil and gas wells that are just being dug, sales is the first indication that a company has the capacity to gain market share and eventually turn a profit. A promise of profitability within two to three years is necessary for most investors and analysts to be optimistic about an asset.

Increasing *cash flow* and solid *earnings* growth are the most transparent elements of value. If the asset is an income producer and not a straight appreciation play, you want it to create steady or growing income. Income investors look mostly at this number; they want to make sure that this cash is paid out directly to them, in the form of dividends or disbursements or rental checks. *Dividend and yield* metrics are vital to the income investor. This is the opposite of a growth investor, who is also looking at earnings, but who wants that cash pumped back into the asset in the form of retained earnings, in order to help it build and grow market share and sales and a higher future value.

Price/Earnings Multiple

The asset's earnings or cash flow drives the price of the asset in that the value is often measured as a multiple of those earnings or cash flow. When earnings are used, this is called the *price/earnings (P/E) multiple.* This is a very helpful measurement for comparing assets within the same sector or class and might be the most famous multiple of all—as far as famous multiples go. It's even printed in the daily newspapers for publicly traded stocks.

To calculate the P/E multiple, divide the price of the asset by the income. This multiple is most commonly used for public companies and private businesses, but it works for other assets, too, like real estate. In fact, you can compare income-producing properties by figuring out the P/E, or, more accurately, the P/CF (price/cash flow). If a multiunit house can sell for $100,000 and produces $20,000 of income for its owner a year, then the price/cash-flow multiple is 5. Some people even call this the EBITDA multiple, but again, these are all variations on a theme.

The most important thing to remember about P/Es, like most numbers used for valuation, is that they are relevant only insofar as they are relative. Saying that an asset has a P/E of 7 is useless unless you know that the average P/E in that asset class is 10. All that P/Es allow investors to do is create a number with which to compare assets—period. An investor is looking at an asset's relative valuation in order to evaluate whether it is overvalued, fairly valued, or under-valued relative to its peer group. An asset with a P/E multiple that is lower than the average P/E in that asset class is said to be "at a dis-count" to the other assets in its class or with which it competes. An asset with a P/E multiple that is higher than the average P/E in its asset class is said to be "at a premium."

Value investors seek out assets that are at a discount and then try to determine whether that discount is warranted or not. Sometimes the market prices something at a discount because it just plain stinks compared to the other assets in its class. The same is true of an asset that is at a premium to others; it might be just way better. To value investors, these weaknesses in the discounted asset may scream opportunity. To growth investors who see an asset trading at a pre-mium, that strength may scream threat. It's all in the perspective of the investor. And that's why valuation is subjective, because potential plays a huge part, and potential is subjective.

There's a famous story of a publicly traded company that was estab-lishing its value for possible acquisition. The management, of course, was arguing that the company's P/E should be at a premium to those of the other companies in this particular industry because it was a supe-rior company. The market bought the argument and pushed the price up so that the price/earning multiple reflected this thought, creating a relatively high P/E and a high purchase price for the acquisition. As the purchase was pending, the spouse of one of the executives and biggest stockholders initiated divorce proceedings and asked for half of the executive's assets. The divorce lawyers did their own due diligence on the value of the stock, using the company's recent valuation as part of their research. Let's just say that the executive had a new argument for why the P/E might be, in this case, a little high.

The Ratios

We have already summarized the *return on investment (ROI)* measurement, a ratio that is used in many valuations. Investors use a number of similar ratios, most of which are derived from the income statement, balance sheet, and cash-flow statement. Some ratios use numbers within a single statement; some jump between statements.

For example, three ratios that jump between the income statement and the balance sheet are the earning power ratios:

1. Sales/assets ratio (the ability of assets to generate sales)
2. Gross profit/assets ratio
3. Net income/assets ratio

An example of a ratio that involves only the balance sheet is the liquidity ratio. This is also called the "current ratio." To get this ratio, current assets are divided by current liabilities. The liquidity ratio—current assets/current liabilities—involves only the balance sheet.

Current assets are those assets that can be converted to cash in less than one year. They include cash, cash equivalents, accounts receivable, some inventory items, and certain marketable securities, like stocks. The current liabilities are the short-term liabilities, those due within a year. The current ratio indicates the business's ability to deal with its short-term debt given the assets it generates or sustains in that same period.

There are dozens of possible ratios to look at. And each industry and asset has specific types. There are ratios on how many times inventory turns a year. There are ratios to help you consider how well the debt is being leveraged against the asset. There are profitability ratios, like the earnings-to-equity ratio, or return on equity (ROE), which is a good measure of efficiency. The dividend yield is another ratio which is the payout per share divided by the cost of owning that share and measures actual cash out from that share.

Book value is the do-re-mi of valuation in a way because it really starts at the very beginning. Literally, it means the value of the left-hand side of the balance sheet. Short-term assets like cash and stocks are shown at their current value. Long-term assets like land and factories are shown at the price at which they were bought. This is the asset's intrinsic value. In bankruptcies and foreclosures, an asset is usually sold at its book value. There are investors who focus only on acquiring assets at a discount to their intrinsic value, which means that they are buying them under book value because they're going to take care of some pending problem, like huge debt or a legal liability.

Hidden Numbers

Within each industry, there are always specific items to look for. When you're considering an asset class like collectibles, you're going to analyze criteria that someone interested in commodities would never think of. It takes experience and sector expertise to know what to look for and ask the right questions. In some businesses the pension plan is underfunded and in others there are excessive inventory levels. For some real estate properties the building is for sale but the land on which it is located is not. Sometimes there is a lot of cash on the balance sheet, and that's a good thing, and sometimes a lot of cash is an indicator of a problem for that business. Some debt levels would kill one asset but would make another thrive. The right answers are there, but the wrong questions can get in the way of finding them. Experience, and help from your team, is the most efficient path to asking the right questions.

Comparable Analysis

If you accept the idea that valuation is subjective and relative, and definitely not objective or absolute, then you are already way ahead of the game. In doing valuations, set up a chart to view a comparison of the financials across the asset's comparables group. The first and most difficult part of that exercise is determining the comparables group. There are investment banks that charge huge fees just to figure out a comparables list.

Some attempts are easier than others. For example, chances are that you can compare Burger King to McDonald's, Wendy's, and Arby's, but even then these companies may have certain assets or divisions that prevent them from being pure comparables. For many real estate properties, brokers will have already created a list of comparables and have evaluated, or will help you evaluate, the relative value of the property based on those comparables.

There are other investments where a list of comparables has not or cannot be made, or a valuation has not been done, particularly when

it comes to private equity ventures. Even
within some obvious comparable groups,
there can be discrepancies like lack of geographic distribution or different product
offerings that affect the comparison. Yet,

> *Close enough is
> good enough in
> comparable analysis.*

even when you are lacking a list of obvious comparables, this is still
one of the best exercises in valuation. The truth is, nothing in life is
truly identical to any other thing, so for all intents and purposes, close
enough is good enough in comparable analysis.

In building this analysis, find the ratios and quantitative factors
that each industry or sector uses to measure its comparables. Finding
these metrics is easier than you think. Any lawyer or accountant in the
industry should know the relevant factors, and may even have comparable lists that he or she put together in previous due diligence exercises. Research reports on public companies will also list metrics; these
can be found through Internet searches and some of the other sources
I mentioned in Chapter 6.

In any valuation process, the smart investor looks not only at
comparables, but at the asset's and the asset class's history and cycles.
Tracking the ups and downs of where an asset has been helps to
anticipate potential fluctuations going forward.

Valuation and the Investor

There are asset classes that it's best not to consider because it's difficult to understand their value proposition. That's okay. The incredi-
ble selection of available assets affords you this luxury. If you choose
an asset class that's a little unusual as compared to the more common assets, like commodities or collectibles, it's your responsibility
to learn how to value these assets in their own unique way.

The methods for valuing assets vary from investor to investor and industry to industry. In some asset classes, such as the public stock and bond markets, the valuations are almost done for you, because there is a public price at which people are buying and selling. In addition, Wall Street has professionals who value stocks and bonds, and the public is privy to much of this information. Equity research analysts are paid to predict share prices and recommend whether investors should buy, sell, or hold onto stocks. These predictions are made using the same criteria that most investors, including me, use to value assets.

The advantage of doing the valuations yourself or with some assistance from colleagues on your team is the same one that you have when you invest directly in assets: any bias is yours. Value is subjective, and many factors come into play. When you are evaluating if an investment is right for you, you want that evaluation to be based on the clearest, most transparent information that you can get. The straightest line to that information is a direct one from you to it.

> *The straightest line to important information about the value of your asset is a direct line from you to it.*

As with due diligence, you want to get help when you perform valuations. To this day, I compare my numbers against those of others to get a more objective analysis. In most cases, you are going to be given a value that has already been established by the seller, and you will compare your valuation to that. It's also important to remember that finding immediate value is not the be-all and the end-all of purchasing an asset. The idea that one buyer can bring a potential improvement to an asset while another buyer cannot lies at the root of an investment decision—sometimes value and price have nothing to do with each other.

The Risk Factor

Once you've completed the quantitative and qualitative valuation, it's time to build in the variables that can affect your results. These variables are known as *risk*. Managing risk is as important as seeking reward. As you learn more about the assets in which you are investing, your overall risk will be reduced. Experience, education, and team—these factors all help you to learn about the asset and thus reduce the risk. But that's only interesting, not helpful, unless you know exactly what investors mean by risk. As you lead your wealth, you must always factor in and manage the other side of reward. Understanding the specific risks in your asset is just as important as valuation in deciding what investments are right for you.

> *Managing risk is as important as seeking reward. As you lead your wealth, you must always factor in and manage the other side of reward.*

8

Risk

Win More, Lose Less

Investing in anything is risky. Life is risky; jobs are risky—everything has a certain level of risk. Just as some things in life seem to have higher risk factors than others, so do some investments. Detecting the levels and realities of those risks is the number one priority of any wealth builder.

Every investment opportunity needs to be specifically and purposefully considered.

As we've discussed, every investment opportunity is different, and both the attributes and the future potential of any such opportunity need to be specifically and purposefully considered. For example, oil and gas takes patience. Such investments can take anywhere from six months to five years to yield a profit, but once they do, the returns can be fantastic—up to 50 percent, and sometimes more. Yet oil and gas can also be a kind of crapshoot in a way that a steady Treasury bond yielding 3 percent a year never will be.

In assessing risk, it's the unasked questions—the assumptions—that create the greatest problems.

I've found that in assessing risk, it's the unasked questions—the assumptions—that create the greatest problems. In investing, what you don't know can in fact hurt you. You need to know the right questions to ask and learn how to identify potential risk in the asset you're considering. Experience is the best teacher—yours, that of your team, and that of your network in the asset class being considered. Once again, it's all about being a team-made millionaire. Investing is no place for a lone ranger.

Risk is *only* your failure to educate yourself around an opportunity. As with due diligence and valuation, there is a vocabulary surrounding the risk conversation. The point of this chapter is to introduce you to the world of risk.

Types of Risk

In investing, an asset is susceptible to several types of risk. There's the intrinsic risk of the asset itself, there's the economic risk of the revenue and earnings model upon which that asset is contingent, and there's the risk of the industry at that time, not to mention the macroeconomic climate.

Risk is only your failure to educate yourself around an opportunity.

Each type of risk is discussed below with an example to illustrate its main point. In this discussion, the investment is in a mobile home park outside of Atlanta, Georgia.

Product Risk

Product risk is inherent in the concept or offering itself. The attributes and characteristics of the product or service are analyzed in terms of their reliability, sustainability, and demand, among other criteria. Rule 1 in product risk is that if you don't understand it, don't buy it. Entering into a venture without really understanding it is similar to the park-and-pray way of investing, and there's no room for park and pray in the Wealth Cycle. One way to investigate product risk is to check

> *Rule 1 in product risk is that if you don't understand it, don't buy it.*

the references or track record of the investment's management—for example, the previous development projects of a contractor.

Product Risk Example

The 20-acre mobile home park has a newly developed infrastructure of electricity and water that is subject to the testing and requirements of the county's environmental and planning and zoning boards. While the management team is confident that the developers are reliable, there is no guarantee that this infrastructure will comply with regulations or fully support the needs of the park's residents.

Economic Risk

Investigations of economic risk assess the numbers necessary for the asset to survive and thrive. Another consideration is whether the investment itself increases or decreases the inherent risk. For example, investing $100,000 in one oil and gas well is highly risky; Investing $100,000 in 40 wells is much more likely to return a strong profit.

Economic Risk Example

The mobile home park consists of 500 mobile homes, and breakeven is contingent on at least 70 percent of the homes being rented at any given time. There are no additional revenue streams for the park at this time, making profitability dependent solely on rentals.

Industry Risk

Industry risk involves the market in which the asset competes. Investigations of industry risk attempt to discern how well the asset can do given competition, industry cycles, and market demand, to name a few factors.

Industry Risk Example

Any rental real estate is a risky proposition, and the rental market in this suburb has had extensive development in the last few years. The management team, however, does not believe that the market has peaked, or even neared maturity, and there is no other mobile home park within 20 miles of this property. Management is confident that there is primary demand for mobile homes that is not being met by the traditional housing market.

Environmental Risk

Investigations of environmental risk measure how susceptible the investment is to the economic climate, demographic shifts, world events, and natural disasters. If, for example, a real estate property is on the Gulf Coast, hurricanes would be a big risk. These hurricanes would affect neighboring markets as well if they led to an inflow of people leaving the disaster area and looking for homes. Immigration is another macro event that can affect a given market. Employment numbers, pricing of raw material, and political movements can all affect an investment. The chamber of commerce can be a good source of information on historical trends, and you can do a basic Web search on the area as well.

Environmental Risk Example

The mobile home park is situated on a swathe of land outside of Atlanta. Traditionally, this area has not been particularly affected by natural disasters, but a wave of immigration into Atlanta has pushed the population outward. The influx of low-wage laborers may increase the demand for housing.

The Universe of Risk

The preceding provides a general overview of risk and how it's presented. Most assets have more specific risk factors that investors need to consider. The universe of possible risks is endless, and it would be impossible to list all the risks that an investor should consider. The example should help you understand the big categories and how they're often presented.

Given how wide the world of risk can be, I can't be completely inclusive here, but let's look at some key risk factors. It's important to note that considering risk is the investors' responsibility, not the responsibility of the seller of the asset. Though there may be a number of risk factors involved in any venture, it takes only one to cause a partial or total loss of one's investment.

> *It takes only one risk factor to cause a partial or total loss of one's investment.*

Risk Factors

The purpose of this section is to get your thoughts percolating about the possible risks and the areas in which perils and hazards could rear their ugly heads. At the very least, these are issues you should consider and questions you should raise.

Valuation Risks

As we have learned, valuation is both objective and subjective. At the end of the day, an asset is worth only what someone else will pay for it. If you underestimated the value, others may outbid you for the asset.

> **An asset is worth only what someone else will pay for it.**

If you overestimated the value, your great deal may turn into a dog when you try to sell. It's also important to remember that risk and reward are usually directly correlated. Higher risk often means higher reward, and vice versa. And although you can manage and reduce risk, your valuation of a high-reward venture must include a degree-of-difficulty factor. The more data you collect, the more accurately you can calculate risk. Due diligence isn't conducted to avoid risk, but to gain a clear picture of what you're getting into.

Financing Risks

This gets to the very heart of investing, because these risks are those involved in financing an asset and are not about the asset itself. Issues that can arise include the following:

1. Insufficient funds are raised, so that there is not enough money to keep the investment going throughout the time required to get to breakeven.

2. There is no near-term market for the investment, meaning that there is no exit strategy, no place to sell, no liquidity for these shares, no demand, and so on.

3. There is a large amount of debt in the ownership structure that is given priority payment over the investors' shares, i.e., it is senior.

4. Parts of the asset itself are being used to collateralize those loans. That is, if all doesn't go well, you could lose the asset.

5. Shareholders' interests are diluted when more money needs to be raised.

Operations Risks

The risks pertaining to how the asset actually functions can come from anywhere. If the asset is new, there will not be any experience to prove its viability, and if it is established, there might be some skeletons rattling in the closet. One way to check into these possibilities is to have conversations with management, employees, or laborers involved with the asset. You might even take a few line workers to lunch.

Strategy and Modeling Risks

Sometimes the very idea that forms the foundation of the asset is weak. For example,

1. Certain marketing strategies are based on traditional patterns of consumer behavior that are changing too quickly to capture.

2. The asset is too dependent on a particular supply or demand channel that has become obsolete.

3. The revenue model is subject to the ebb and flow of the global economy.

4. Competitors can create new and better products, lower prices, and so on, to the detriment of the asset.

5. Adverse conditions in general could rock the asset.

Management Risks

The asset could be solely dependent on a single, superstar leader, and any threats to that leadership could vaporize the value of the asset. Or there could be huge unknowns about a new management team that is unproven in this asset class—or the team is proven in this asset class, but not as leaders. Worse, the leadership's attention could be divided between this asset and others, or it could have other conflicts of interest that are not clear at first.

Reducing Risk

The factors just listed are only a small sliver of the possible risks that can arise when investing. The fact that Wealth Cycle Investing works off direct asset allocation has many advantages, one of them being that the market for direct placement deals tends to be inefficient. There's just not enough transparency and information flowing about. This is an advantage, because it means that smart investors can get a better risk/reward ratio by really concentrating on due diligence, valuation, and risk assessment efforts.

It's possible that some people may see the responsibility for due diligence and risk assessment as a disadvantage of this model. I have to disagree. Putting these responsibilities in the hands of a financial planner may be easier, but it's not secure. Almost every asset, investment, and market has been subject to bad cycles and pitfalls. I'd rather at least have looked under the rug or in the closet myself. It is important to also note that most assets are susceptible to risks that cannot be predicted, or sometimes even appreciated, by management or investors. Unforeseen risks can be endless, which is why investors can never remove all the risks, even if they think they have. But there are several things that Wealth Cycle investors can do to manage risk.

ACTION STEPS FOR MANAGING RISK

- Collecting an experienced, reliable, and honest team
- Educating oneself about each and every investment
- Learning the vocabulary of each investment and its asset class
- Getting comfortable with the numbers
- Communicating well and often
- Building one's own experience and confidence by taking action
- Narrowing in on specific, targeted, direct investments
- Achieving expertise, through team and knowledge, in each asset
- Diversifying into other assets, sectors, or industries
- Sticking to one's Money Rules
- Doing due diligence for each and every investment
- Maintaining one's management systems
- Keeping legal contracts current
- Ensuring complete and detailed financial records
- Continuously putting revenues and expenditures into entities
- Pursuing proper tax strategies

All of these activities will help you better manage your risk. As you can see, these responsibilities—leadership, teamwork, conditioning, and entities—are some of the building blocks of the Wealth Cycle. These skills are requirements for a Wealth Cycle investor and vital catalysts for increasing the reward and reducing the risk of every single investment you make.

In the next few chapters, I'm going to dive deeper into a few of the investments in which I'm involved to give you an idea of what high-reward investing is about. These assets include real estate, private equity business ventures, and other alternative assets that asset addicts like me adore.

9

Real Estate

Location, Land, and Leverage

t's no secret that real estate is a favorite asset class of the wealthy. In fact, there are professional wealth-building experts who talk about real estate as though it's the be-all and the end-all, and from their books and lectures, you'd swear that it's the only game in town. It's not. It's a great asset class, and it's a big portion of my portfolio, but it's getting smaller.

While real estate can be a terrific investment for both appreciation and cash flow, providing both growth and income investors a little happiness along the way, it's a play that's got a catch. If it's held as an income asset, you cannot obtain a steady cash flow from real estate without good management, effortless internal operations, and a distinct and consistent marketing strategy. If it's held as an appreciation asset, macroeconomic issues such as demographic and economic shifts, not to mention natural disasters, can blindside you.

When these problems arise, the efforts don't pay off in either cash flow or appreciation. Those are some of the risks. The catch is that in real estate, you almost always have to be an active investor, closely linked to your field partners and your team. If you choose to go into a real estate deal as a passive investor, with your money being the OPM (other people's money), then, as with any passive investment, you must have an experienced, proven team led by an experienced, trustworthy, aggressive, and resourceful field partner. When you find the right field partners and the right markets, you can have a cash-and-appreciation cow.

I like real estate as an asset class, and while there's no such thing as a sure thing, I do like the surer things. That's why I'm usually in the streets alongside my real estate investments. I scout out the markets and find field partners who are located in the area where I want to invest, know all the players, and have done this kind of deal before. Let's look at a real estate deal as an initial entry into assets through Jed Stone's experience.

Getting into Assets

After spending time on his Cash Machine and setting up a corporate life, Jed Stone was ready to move into assets building. I suggested that real estate would be a good first deal that would build his level of experience. To begin his education, Jed started reading up on the industry, collecting data, and becoming familiar with the vocabulary of this asset class. Then Jed reached out to real estate professionals and investors in Boston and followed them around, listening in on negotiations and watching them do deals.

By the time Jed had saved some money in his Wealth Account, he was ready for the next step in his education: action. We wanted to get him in on a deal by offering experienced players a small sum of money in return for a small piece of the action. This would allow him to buy a passive investor seat at the table—to look, to listen, and to learn.

As I did with Dee Newton, I connected Jed with a field partner of mine who was buying houses that generated monthly cash flow. The market was bread-and-butter houses. This field partner had discovered these houses and had developed a team that consisted of a trustworthy property manager, a reliable handyman, and a local rental agent. There would be no appreciation on these properties, even if they were fixed up. The demographics of the market gave us reason to believe that the houses would attract a steady stream of renters. The final factor was that the houses were inexpensive enough to do the fixes, pay to have them managed, charge inexpensive rent, and still make a nice monthly profit.

The houses needed a little bit of renovation here and there, but the field partner had a property manager who took care of this, and also marketed to potential tenants and did the monthly collection of rent. As I mentioned in Dee's example, the homes cost $45,000 each. The investment that my field partner required for one of these houses was $6,000, of which $4,500 was the down payment. The balance was loan fees, closing costs, and the costs of some minor repairs. By the time he was ready to jump into the deal, Jed had $3,000 available in his Wealth Account. He knew a friend of his who would be interested in going in on the other $3,000.

We created a Wealth Cycle Investing Worksheet that allowed Jed to educate himself about, and then evaluate, this opportunity.

Jed bought one of these cash-flow houses. The $3,000 that Jed spent could have been his tuition for an adult-extension course in

---

JED STONE'S
WEALTH CYCLE INVESTING WORKSHEET

ASSET UNDER CONSIDERATION:
A small three-bedroom, one-bath bread-and-butter house

CONTACT PERSON(S):
One of Loral's field partners

SETUP

SOURCE OF FUNDS:

Wealth Account   **OPM**   *OPI*   *Bank*   *Loan Restructuring of Other Asset*

Needed $6,000; Of this, $3,000 would come from Wealth Account, $3,000 from friend

---

ENTITIES:

Jed set up an LLC to oversee, manage, and build these investments. The LLC, owned 50–50 with his friend, would take title to the asset after closing.

Separately, Jed also established a trust that would oversee all of Jed's businesses and ensure additional protection.

FORECASTING:

Depreciation and other expenditures directly related to the business of investing in these assets would be funneled into the LLC. Revenue from this asset would be transferred into holding accounts (corporate Wealth Accounts), as well as into a debt management plan.

Revenue from Jed's Cash Machine was also funneled into the LLC, via a loan from the Cash Machine's holding account, in order to make additional investments in real estate.

—MONEY RULES—

ROI GOAL AND PROJECTED

Jed's Freedom Day goal was $1,000,000 in invested assets and $10,000 a month in passive income. Eventually, Jed's ROI requirements would be in the 10 percent range. But at this point he had no assets and was just building his Cash Machine. Jed needed aggressive, above-market ROIs.

At $1,200 a year (that's $2,400 a year minus half to his friend) on his $3,000 investment, this asset would generate an annual ROI of 33 percent.

CASH FLOW	**APPRECIATION**
100%	*0%*
	These homes generally do not appreciate.
ACTIVE	**PASSIVE**
	Jed needed to learn from others, and a seat at the table was all he was looking for at this point in time.

DIVERSIFICATION

Allocation   Risk/Reward   Exit Strategy

ALLOCATION: *Jed's Financial Baseline reflected assets of $5,000, all in cash. Jed would begin his asset allocation by investing in real estate. Eventually, this bucket would represent both income-generating and appreciating properties.*

RISK/REWARD: *This cash-flow-generating asset promised to be in the middle range of the risk/reward allocation that Jed was building.*

EXIT STRATEGY: *This is an income-generating asset that can be viewed as an annuity that, with consistent maintenance and intermittent improvements, could continue in perpetuity. An alternative strategy could be sale of the asset for the present value of the annuity at that time.*

—TEAM—

LEADER: *Jed Stone*
FIELD PARTNER: *From Loral's Big Table*
MENTORS: *Uncle's friend, a local real estate developer*
PROFESSIONALS: *Lawyer, accountant, entity specialist, bookkeeper*
UTILITY PLAYERS: *A housecleaner at $10 an hour to give Jed the hours he needs to build his assets.*
OTHERS: *Field partner's team of property manager, agents, handyman*

—DUE DILIGENCE—

DATA	DISCUSSION	DISCOVERY	DIAGNOSIS	DECISION
Texts and workbooks	Uncle	Internet video tour	**Strength:** Comfort level with the field partner's track record (the numbers made this appealing)	Yes
Trades	Mentor	Trip to view asset with field partner		
Internet	Experts			
Seminars	Field partner		**Weaknesses:** Concerns about the continuing market demand for rentals	

real estate. Researching the possibility of a real live deal, and perhaps even saying yes to the deal and doing it, has got to be at least as good an education, if not better, as the real-estate course. If the money's lost, it's tuition. Then again, there's the upside.

The house drew rent of $695 a month. The PITI (principal, interest, taxes, and insurance) plus management fees equaled $495. This gave Jed and his friend $200 a month in cash flow. Jed's personal cash-flow statement would reflect half of this:

Source of cash: $347.50
Use of cash: $247.50
Monthly cash flow: $100

That's a nice return. It also implied full recoupment of the investment in less than three years, and free cash thereafter. Of course, this was contingent on several factors, including upkeep of the property, consistent demand, and his team staying on the job.

As you may have guessed, when an opportunity like this surfaces, most investors do not buy just one home. For example, Dee Newton bought 10 right off the bat. However, although this was an attractive deal, Jed was a first-time investor, and a first-time investor needs to have restraint. For Jed, this was about practice and learning. This was a good way for him to get into assets, because he could do it for $3,000.

Jed made $100 a month in passive income, a cool $1,200 a year that went right back into his Wealth Account. Jed was able to retain most of this income. He did this by setting up an LLC that oversaw and managed his investments. His expenditures included his trip to check out the asset, his meetings with the field partner, his research, and other costs, including typical office supplies such as his telephone, photocopying, and expenses for meetings with people such as his OPM partner. In addition, Jed realized depreciation from this asset, another significant expenditure that offset some of the revenue.

As you probably know, depreciation on income-producing real estate is a tax-deductible expenditure. This is usually the price of the property less the value of the land, since land cannot be depreciated, divided by the life of the property, which under IRS rules is 27.5 years for residential real estate. In Jed's case, the price of the asset was $45,000, of which 80 percent, or $36,000, was the house and 20 percent, or $9,000, was the land. Since land cannot be depreciated, the $36,000 was divided by 27.5 years, which meant that he and his friend could deduct $1,309 a year in total, or $654 each. They were collecting $2,400 a year in cash, or $1,200 each. Obviously, this amount was significant. They'd each pay taxes on less than half the cash flow that they actually received—and that would be before deducting other relevant expenses.

Jed now found himself with an asset and a team. Like most deals, this team required different people who brought different things to the table. Jed and his friend brought money. Others brought credit, others experience, and still others the muscle, time, and energy in the streets, including due diligence discovery assistance, relationships, and community goodwill. Since he had no experience and little knowledge, it was imperative that Jed have a solid team for his first deal. This made it an excellent learning vehicle for him.

Having had experience with this type of asset, Jed was eager to try it on his own. His grandparents were from a small city in upstate New York that seemed to him to be very similar to the town where he'd bought the bread-and-butter cash-flow house. His grandparents' town was neither booming nor trendy, but it seemed to be experiencing some growth after a decade of decline, and his grandparents had observed that demand for housing was up. Jed decided to take a three-day weekend there and scope out the opportunities.

Jed checked out the chamber of commerce projections for new businesses coming in and liked the growth that he saw. He also went to the board of education and learned that it was projecting a need for more schools. He then went to a few real estate brokers and asked if they could connect him with any professional real estate investors in town. Jed was introduced to some, and when he found one whose track record was solid, he shared his idea. Jed was going to raise money that he could use to buy several homes, overseen by a field partner and his team who wanted some skin in the game, or sweat equity.

The investor agreed to become Jed's field partner on the deal. He had a team of lawyers and professional property managers, and he chose a broker who could help find what Jed wanted. This led to a day of looking at properties.

Jed saw dozens of homes that fit the criteria he'd established. He took the deal sheets home to Boston and met with others. The mentor he'd found at the bank was interested and talked to some of his friends. Jed and his mentor set up the LLC and got the paperwork in motion. To Jed's excitement, he was soon able to raise enough money to make the down payment on 15 homes in this upstate market. Jed then went back to his field partner, who connected him with his real estate lawyer, who connected him to a local bank. Happy to have Jed's funds, the field partner put up his own credit to get the loans. They drew up the paperwork. Jed also connected with the others on the field partner's team, including the property managers. He made his field partner a sweat equity partner, and the LLC was created and the investments made. Since the field partner could benefit from the cash flow and the appreciation, he looked after these assets as if they were his own—because they were.

By the time Jed was in his second year of investing, he began to see income from his homes in upstate New York. The 15 homes in upstate New York cost investors $6,000 each and were paid for with $90,000 of OPM. They were valued at an average of $50,000 each, and his team made a 10 percent down payment on each. The investors put in $6,000 for 90 percent ownership in each home, giving Jed and his field partner the other 10 percent ownership, as well as $600 per home, as a fee for finding, rehabbing, marketing, and managing the homes. After monthly expenses, the investors realized $180 monthly cash flow on each home, and Jed and his field partner realized $20 per home.

Let's look at his Gap Analysis at this point.

JED STONE'S GAP ANALYSIS		
FREEDOM DAY GOALS		
● $1,000,000 in invested assets	● A business of owning gyms	
● $10,000/month in passive income	● No full-time job	

REVENUE	ASSETS
CASH MACHINE:	
$2,000/month	
PASSIVE INCOME CASH FLOW:	
$100/month cash flow	$3,000 in one cash-flow house
$150/month fee	Monthly fees and up-front fees for each of 15 homes
$4,500 in upfront fees	

PREVIOUS FINANCIAL BASELINE

PRETAX INCOME: $3,667/MONTH		ASSETS:	$5,000
EXPENDITURES: $2,500/MONTH		LIABILITIES:	$7,000
		NET WORTH:	−$2,000

CURRENT FINANCIAL BASELINE

PRETAX INCOME: $5,617/MONTH		ASSETS:	$87,500
EXPENDITURES: $3,000/MONTH		LIABILITIES:	$73,750
		NET WORTH:	$13,750

● Skill set: organization, communications, workout discipline

● Assets increased by the value of the bread-and-butter home, $45,000, and the 5 percent of the 15 upstate New York homes, valued at $50,000 each, for a total of $37,500.

● His liabilities were the commercial debt on the bread-and-butter home, which was $40,000, and his 5 percent share of the liability on the upstate New York homes, which was $45,000 each, for a total of $33,750. We used money from his Cash Machine to pay off the credit card debt and the loan to his sister, leaving Jed with only good debt.

Good debt is debt that is leveraged against performing assets. Bad debt is debt that is used for perishable items; it usually takes the form of credit card debt. With the cash from his Cash Machine and some of the passive income, Jed eliminated his bad debt, leaving him with only good debt.

With his Cash Machine and his assets, Jed was now collecting an additional $2,250 a month in revenue. In addition, although he'd used much of the Cash Machine money to manage his debt and research his wealth, he had almost all of his $4,500 in the real estate LLC's holding account, or corporate Wealth Account, ready for investments. After paying down his bad debt, Jed could get the Cash Machine money into Wealth Accounts as well. About six months into the second year of his Wealth Cycle, Jed had $10,000 designated for more investments.

Although I recommended that Jed keep his job while he built his Wealth Cycle, if he kept this up, he'd have to reconsider that. As mentioned earlier, unless a person is a professional real estate investor as defined by the IRS, the amount that person can take in depreciation deductions is limited. People who keep W-2 jobs while accelerating the Wealth Cycle and increasing real estate assets and entities will end up straddling two worlds and losing valuable deductible depreciation dollars.

First Steps

Real estate is a good first asset deal. You can look at a small or accessible property; decide how to restructure some existing assets or use the money you've built up in your Wealth Account; set up your entity; ramp up the learning curve on structuring a deal, both legally and financially; and learn how to run your business and build your team—all for a low entry fee and the possibility of a nice upside. In addition, you'll learn how to utilize depreciation in your tax strategies as well as forecast other expenditures that are related directly to this new business venture.

Although eventually you can have thousands of dollars a month coming into your mailbox just from real estate, real estate is a slow game. This first asset deal of yours may not be a big boon to your Wealth Cycle yet. You'll start with investigation and research, building your team and establishing the systems and structures to manage the properties, but this work will be hardest the first time.

For this first asset deal, I'm going to reiterate my philosophy of "not in your own backyard." Many owners and investors do just that: they start in their own backyard. This can work well if you live in bread-and-butter America. But if you live in a growing, booming town, with an expanding and appreciating market, then most real estate opportunities are probably pure appreciation plays. Fair market rents will probably be less than your monthly mortgage, maintenance, and interest costs. That means you'll be underwater every month, and that's not all right. Your investments shouldn't cost you money.

That's why I say *you should live where you want to live and invest where it makes sense.*

I live on a mountainside, deep in a forest, overlooking a lake. It's nice. But it's not where I invest. My investment real estate portfolio extends across the country, in almost two dozen states, through a web of field partners and real estate professionals. This is also part of my diversification strategy.

The weather disasters that have pummeled the globe in the past few years are a reminder that geographical diversification is paramount. You cannot control or predict disaster. I've lost investments in floods and hurricanes, but these losses have been balanced by wins in other parts of the world. Fortunately, in those areas that were hit hard, my field partners picked themselves up again fast, and my team and I have been involved in helping those areas rebuild.

Within real estate, I also have diversification by asset class. This is accomplished through investments in properties that range from land and preconstruction to huge residential and commercial properties. In order to pursue this type of diversification in real estate assets that generate high returns, real estate investors require reliable teams. The team provides the legwork to create the diversification and the experience to reduce risk. Real estate investing requires finding the experts, leading the team, and driving your wealth.

Opportunities in Real Estate

The single-family, cash-flow-generating home is just one example of a viable real estate property. I look at all types of real estate. Here's a sample.

Residential Real Estate

Residential real estate is properties with four units or less; those with five units or more are considered commercial real estate. Residential real estate can be acquired through many sources. The most common is the Multiple Listing Service (MLS). This is a list compiled by real estate professionals that gives all of the available properties listed by Realtors in a certain area. These listings are used by most Realtors, are up-to-date and inclusive, and can be found on the Web. Another source is the For Sale By Owner (FSBO) listings, which are not included in the MLS. Look in the newspapers or drive around, because not all of these properties are on the Web. I also look for foreclosures by banks, the Housing and Urban Development (HUD), and the Veteran's Administration (VA). Even other investors can be a source of deals from time to time. The most efficient searches are done through the Internet. Or hire people to do research in the country recorder's office and find the preforeclosures listings.

Land

There are numerous opportunities in land. These range from small residential lots to thousands of acres of untitled land. Size and zoning will dictate price and development opportunities, and either you develop the land yourself or you sell it to a developer who does the work. Obviously, the best land is in areas where there is growth. If you're interested in land, I've found that small parcels in subdivisions are a good place to start. There are always less desirable parcels that were passed over by the first buyers. Once the initial wave of acquisition passes, the developer is usually eager to move on to the next project, and these parcels can often be acquired at a discount. As the surrounding properties appreciate, so will the remnant parcel. Another way to try to make a profit on land is to improve the land and make it more valuable. This includes bringing utilities to the site, grading the site in preparation for development, and enhancing the site with landscaping. There are also title and development improvements that can be made, such as zoning, subdivision, planning approvals, leasing, and financing. Anything that creates an immediate opportunity for developers helps sell the property.

Multitenant Buildings

General use structures, such as warehouse buildings and multitenant structures, are appealing for both office and retail demand. The more general the use, the greater the demand. One of my favorite investments of this type is the miniwarehouse. The demand for additional storage space continues to grow, and these properties are very attractive development projects.

Real Estate Options

There are many ways to play real estate as an asset. Not only is the range of assets wide, but there are tools within the asset, such as real estate options, that can generate cash flow for your Wealth Cycle. Though they are not the best step for a beginner, options provide a good way for someone without much up-front money to get in on an asset and create a quick turnaround.

An option is the right to buy a property or asset at a certain price during a certain time period. You're probably familiar with stock options. Options are available on many assets, and they offer a way for both the buyer and the seller of the option to make some money. Let's look at buying a real estate option.

If you've done your due diligence on an asset and feel that you can increase the appreciation of that asset within a certain amount of time, then an option is a nice way to leverage a little bit of money for a whole lot of gain. One of my colleagues did this with a large commercial property. A contractor had the right to control the property. After extensive due diligence and the creation of a new marketing strategy for the property, my colleague paid the contractor

$25,000 for the right to purchase the property at a certain price, $200,000, within a certain time frame, one year.

This option, like many, is risky, because if it's not exercised—that is, if my colleague doesn't buy the property within the specified time period—then control goes back to the owner and my colleague loses his $25,000. As you can imagine, you should not enter an option agreement without an end-use plan in place. The deal is complete when the owner of the option finds a buyer who is willing to pay a price greater than the property price plus the option payment, or $225,000. If the price of the commercial real estate has gone way up in that period, either because of the market or because of a repositioning of the property, the owner of the option will benefit. If the option owner can't sell the property for at least $225,000, then he'll lose. My colleague was able to find a buyer who was willing to buy the property for $300,000. This gave him $100,000 return on his $25,000 investment, or $75,000 free and clear. Options are a great way to leverage a little bit of money for a lot of gain. If the price of the underlying asset goes down, the loss is limited to the price of the option.

Options tend to work best when the market is not hot. In an appreciating market, it is not easy to get an owner to lock into a set price. Options also work very well in other assets too, such as land or businesses. One of my colleagues has a strategy of leasing cash-generating retail operations, like Laundromats, for a year, with an option to purchase the operation at the end of the year. He does this to test the reality of the cash flow the owner claims. Talk about due diligence! This is also a good way to work your way into the asset if you don't have a lot of money. If you have an endgame in sight, buying options is a terrific way to leverage your funds.

Selling options is another revenue generator. As a property owner, I've offered many of my renters options to buy. The tenants usually want the options because they may not have the best credit, and this is a good way into ownership for them. The owner sets the option-to-buy price at a level that is fair to the tenant and still desirable to the owner.

The tenant-buyer makes a separate up-front payment as consideration for the purchase option. This is usually around 3 percent of the option-to-buy price. Yet, in my experience, less than one out of five tenants exercise these options. That means that 80 percent of the time I end up keeping the option consideration payment for options that were never exercised. If you're comfortable with the price you've set with the tenant, then selling options and garnering the sure-thing fee and possible sale is a good asset to have in your allocation.

Sealing the Deal

Buying properties is actually the easiest part of real estate investing. Selling them and ensuring a profit is where you must be creative. Of course, the smarter you are on the buy side, the better you'll do on the sell side. The best route to profit is (1) buying right, that is, paying a price on which you know you can make a profit, and (2) buying with a clear plan for an exit strategy.

I call the latter "future pacing." I recommend it for every investment. Future pacing is the ability to look down the road, decide the future goal, and create strategies to produce that result. Let's say you are doing a rehab. The amount of rehab you will do will depend on whether the buyer is another investor, an owner-occupant, or a renter or lease tenant. By looking at it this way, you'll do only the repairs and renovations that match your strategy. The end goal always trumps the process. For example, if you're not finished with the rehab work and an offer is made that matches your goal, you can take the offer and exit the investment even before you finish the work.

The Specifics

Getting into real estate requires specific knowledge. You can and will capture this knowledge during the early stages of your learning by talking to mentors and reading articles from various consumer and trade publications, many of which can be found online; and scouting out opportunities. I'm such a fan of direct action that my colleagues and I even take groups of clients for three days of intensive in-the-streets training, where they get hands-on experience in real deals and learn the spectrum of property acquisition and sales. Collect your knowledge, get a team, set your eyes on some properties, and con-sider making a deal. As with Jed's $3,000 investment, not only might it lead to an upside, but it will give you the best education you can get: experience.

Let's look at another arena for better-than-average returns: pri-vate equity ventures. It's all pretty exciting, and when you take your first step toward financial freedom, you'll see how much fun invest-ing can be.

10

Private Equity Ventures

Making Business Something Personal

Private equity is one of the most lucrative asset classes in which one can invest. Every big company, every new product idea—almost everything in our lives—was, at one time, just an idea in some dreamer's head. It was the courage of the investors who put capital into those dreams that made them possible. New product ideas and private businesses are some of the most exciting, and rewarding, investments that you can make.

Investing in this asset class, *private equity,* is not for the casual investor. Sometimes you're putting money into a concept that's just sketched out on a piece of paper. Investments can range from an invention to a fully functioning business that's recapitalizing to create something better. Equity ventures cover every possible industry and revenue model. By my definition, when we talk about private equity investments, we're talking about the purchase of ownership in any venture that does not have its equity or its debt available on the public markets.

Investors look for either cash flow or appreciation, and sometimes both, in these assets. Usually there are no liquid markets for the equity shares of these assets, so that appreciation has to come through an exit strategy of either a full or partial acquisition or an IPO (initial public offering). I do not consider the purchase of a franchise or entry into multilevel marketing programs to be private equity. And because we're talking about direct asset allocation, I do not consider buying into equity or leveraged buyout funds to be this type of asset either.

I'm currently involved with a number of business ventures, and I like this type of investment for several reasons:

1. **They're tangible.** I can see the idea, and I can see where it has to go to get its just rewards. New ventures are the epitome of having to do the right thing at the right time.
2. **They're exciting.** There's just nothing like seeing something that was nothing become something, or seeing an asset that's a mess get a great team on board, fix its problems, and take off. I always say that with leadership, marketing, sales, and financial experience, we can turn a company for profit.
3. **They're rewarding.** Both cash flow and appreciation can come to you through new ventures. Of the businesses in which I'm currently involved, one is solely an appreciation opportunity. I consider it a pure equity play that will lose money until we exercise the exit strategy, which will probably be an acquisition. Another is a pure cash-flow play, currently enjoying cash flow of 20 to 30 percent a year. I don't see a likely exit strategy that provides any appreciation, unless an investor wishes to pay me some multiple of that cash flow for the right to it. Another will initially have negative cash flow and

then turn positive for a bit, but we'll probably realize the real returns with the sale. And yet another should have both income and growth. There will be cash flow right away and appreciation sometime after that, if the brand equity is built up properly.

4. **They're diverse.** There's a lot of diversification built right into this asset class. There's the variety of

- Returns
- Yields
- Time frames
- Product offerings
- Target markets
- Industries
- Business models

Getting Personal

A phrase that is frequently used in business is "it's not personal; it's just business." I couldn't disagree more. I take business very personally. For example, management and personnel are at the core of every business venture and are key to its success, so I like to know the people who are at the helm of each enterprise. It's important to

Business is personal.

me to understand their qualities and characteristics and feel confident that making the business a success is their priority, too. I like to hear about the day-to-day goings on and have some input into the venture's progress. That's why I find it so hard to just buy a company's stock on the open market. I'm not an *active* investor in all of my business ventures, but I do want to be able to pick up the phone and ask a few questions every once in a while. I can't help myself.

One of the business ventures I recently considered was a new product development company in the video game industry. My strategy looked something like this:

LORAL'S	
WEALTH CYCLE WORKSHEET	

ASSET UNDER CONSIDERATION:
  Ted-Jen, a new product development company in the video gaming industry.

CONTACT PERSON(S):
  Ted G. and Jenny B., managing members of the company

—SETUP—

SOURCE OF FUNDS:

Wealth Account	OPM	OPI	Bank Loan Restructuring of Other Asset

  I would be taking money straight out of my Wealth Account for this investment.

ENTITIES:
  I would set up a new LLC for this.

FORECASTING:
  Perhaps revenue would eventually come into the LLC, but initially, for an estimated first 12 months for sure, there would be none. Initially and going forward, I would have some expenditures. These would be expenses associated with any purchases, time, and efforts I'd make in learning about, and staying on top of, this investment. These might collect as tax loss carry forwards.

—MONEY RULES—

ROI GOAL AND PROJECTED
  This was a pure growth opportunity, and initial cash flow would be zero. I was looking for an investment that would quadruple my money by the projected exit strategy, to take effect in less than five years.

CASH FLOW	**APPRECIATION**
0%	100%

ACTIVE	**PASSIVE**
	I'd have plenty to say, and I'd have a seat on the advisory board, but I'd let the managing members do their job.

DIVERSIFICATION

| Allocation | Risk/Reward | Exit Strategy |

ALLOCATION: *I had nothing in this industry, and I wanted some participation in the media and gaming sector. The time seemed right to consider this sector, given the trends I'd observed.*

RISK/REWARD: *High. New product development is at the high end of the risk/reward spectrum.*

EXIT STRATEGY: *Acquisition. Via sale to a bigger player in the industry.*

—TEAM—

LEADERS: *Loral*

FIELD PARTNERS: *Ted G. and Jenny B.*

MENTORS: *A colleague who'd been in this industry for several years.*

PROFESSIONALS: *Lawyer, accountant, entity specialist, bookkeeper*

UTILITY PLAYERS: *I've got Team Langemeier in every facet of my home and personal life helping me keep my Wealth Cycle spinning.*

—DUE DILIGENCE—

DATA	DISCUSSION	DISCOVERY	DIAGNOSIS	DECISION
The company's materials, other companies' materials, Internet sites on gaming, trade magazines, sector research reports	*Field partner* *Industry experts* *Mentors*	*Meeting with the managing members* *Hands-on look at the concept and prototype*	*Strengths:* *Management* *Ideas* *Weaknesses:* *Technology and the production time frames*	*No*

As much as I liked the management and appreciated the entrepreneur's energy and vision, my due diligence efforts ultimately led me to say no. While the product was exciting and engaging, and seemed to fit the industry demand, the ramp-up period to finished product seemed too long, and I worried about missing the market opportunity. I was also concerned about underfunding in this capitalization. This last consideration is a very important part of the due diligence process. If the company raises $5 million, works hard on the project for two years, and then needs another million to hit the homestretch—well, (1) that's typical, but (2) it creates a need for a second round of financing. This isn't a bad thing, and it does often happen. But it means that management has to either go back to the first investors or do its dog-and-pony show for new investors. Raising capital takes time, money, and management energy, which means taking the focus off developing the actual product. There's also an added degree of risk, which includes everything from changes in the industry to the economic climate. It's best to invest when you know that the asset is fully capitalized (even overcapitalized) so that the product has the best chance of getting to market. This raises another point: you should always know that your stage of financing is in fact financing. Sometimes management is looking for just enough money to get to prototype. This matters in that you need to be aware of the objectives and consequences of your specific investment.

Bringing Your Brain to the Game

As with most investments, when you get into private equity ventures, you can't chase numbers or booms. Just because your friends invested in coffee retail stores several years ago and made a bundle doesn't mean that the outcome will be the same for you. Your objective in private equity is to find the soundest concepts and business models. Too many smart people try to get into the latest and greatest thing as if they were the first to discover it. Almost every market goes through cycles; we've all seen it. The market is born, it grows, it peaks, it weakens, and it ends, perhaps to experience a rebirth, or perhaps never to be heard from again.

In Wealth Cycle Investing, you do not follow wealth, you lead it. I'm very wary of booms and busts, and I don't like to jump on the latest trend. My view is that if everyone's talking about an asset, it's too late. In the example of the video gaming product, the idea was not as hot as the industry for which it was targeted. In this instance, I felt that I was paying a premium for getting in on the glamour of the asset. And I don't like to pay those premiums. Beyond being swayed by an industry or trend, I want to understand a business venture and its concept, and see a clear revenue model that makes sense. I like to see steps and schedules that I know can work.

In educating people about Wealth Cycle Investing, I focus on *sequencing,* which is doing the right thing at the right time. The ability to know what to do when is one of the most important characteristics of good leadership. In buying into a business—more so really than with any other asset—it's important that the sequence of steps in the company's business model makes sense. If a company operating in a market that thrives on fast product life cycles has a product that is perfectly in sync with current market trends but can't get that product onto the shelves quickly, that's not good sequencing—that's a risky investment. I was quick to see this flaw in the gaming investment, and it weighed too heavily on my gut (my best decision-making friend) for me to move ahead.

Another tool for determining the value of an investment is reverse timelines, which entails working backward to see if what needs to be done can be done, much as is done in reverse engineering. I've found sequencing and reverse timelines to be indispensable when assessing new products or business developments.

An Equity Venture for the New Investor

After Mick Buchanan set up his entities and forecasted his revenues and expenditures, he restructured his lazy assets. This included taking $100,000 of equity out of his home and the $40,000 from his mutual funds. He put some of this into 10 real estate properties in the Midwest. He couldn't find a $6,000 per house deal like Jed did, but he did find homes in a small industrial town that cost him $8,000 each and delivered $250 per month cash flow each. Mick earmarked the other $60,000 for an investment in a private equity venture.

I introduced Mick to an opportunity that had surfaced in one of my Big Tables and in which I had invested. Most private equity ventures begin with minimum investments in the $50,000 to $100,000 area, so Mick's investment would be within the appropriate range. But most are for accredited investors, a criterion that Mick hadn't yet attained. With his potential in assets and his ramped-up business, I asked the field partner to consider Mick for one of the 35 slots the SEC (Securities Exchange Commission) allows for nonaccredited investors.

My field partner on this was a business broker who was constantly seeking new ventures. He'd brought a few select ideas to my attention, and one in particular had struck all the right chords: the private-label nutritional products manufacturer that I mentioned in the chapter on due diligence. We drew up a Wealth Cycle Investing Worksheet for Mick to look at this investment.

MICK BUCHANAN'S
WEALTH CYCLE INVESTING WORKSHEET

ASSET UNDER CONSIDERATION:
A manufacturer and distributor in the food and drug industry.

CONTACT PERSON(S):
Big Table business broker

—**SETUP**—

SOURCE OF FUNDS:

Wealth Account   OPM   OPI   ***Restructuring of Other Asset***

Mick would use $60,000 from restructuring his assets.

ENTITIES:
A new LLC

FORECASTING:

The cash flow would go directly to the new entity, and related expenditures would be written off against it. There was no depreciation, as this was not a business that required much capital equipment investment from which Mick could benefit.

—**MONEY RULES**—

ROI GOAL AND PROJECTED

The company already existed, and the field partner was coming in to fix it and make it better. It was already throwing off cash flow, with annual yield in the area of 30 percent, and there was potential for appreciation. The 30 percent annual ROI worked for Mick, and if the exit strategy pushed the overall ROI higher, it would be a happy day.

APPRECIATION	CASH FLOW
50%	50%

ACTIVE	PASSIVE
	Mick was learning, and he knew too little about food or drugs. He also had a field partner on the job 24 hours a day, committed to being CEO.

(continued)

DIVERSIFICATION

Allocation   *Risk/Reward*   *Exit Strategy*

ALLOCATION: *A new business venture was a big leap in asset allocation for Mick, but I liked this play in the food and drug category, given the price/earnings stability of these types of products once they find their place in the market. The fact that the field partner was bringing marketing and product development strategies to increase revenue gave it a value-growth angle that worked well for Mick's strategy.*

RISK/REWARD: *High. The ready cash flow minimized the risk, but this business has to be seen as midrange to high risk. The growth prospects increased the reward, but the risk remained high because of the inherent vulnerabilities of any product or business.*

EXIT STRATEGY: *Initial public offering, merger with a competitor/supply- or demand-side partner, or sale.*

—TEAM—

LEADERS: *Mick*

FIELD PARTNERS: *Big Table business broker*

MENTORS: *FDA specialist, industry experts*

PROFESSIONALS: *Lawyer, accountant, entity specialist, bookkeeper*

UTILITY PLAYERS: *Mick and Mary hired some help at home, and Mick got an intern to help with the Cash Machine.*

—DUE DILIGENCE—

DATA	DISCUSSION	DISCOVERY	DIAGNOSIS	DECISION
Industry and trade research	Field partner	Meetings with the managing members and the current company executives	*Strengths:*	Yes
Company material	Industry experts		Business model	
	Mentors		Management	
	Company executives		R&D team	
			Weakness:	
		Visit to the factory and the retailers that sold the product.	Potential consumer fickleness	

The key due diligence question for Mick was why the field partner thought that he could achieve yields and growth that the former owner had not. This is always a concern with a value buy because sometimes there's a reason that the price isn't at a premium. After many discussions with the field partner and the scientists at the company, Mick and I were convinced that their ideas for new product growth and better marketing strategies were sound. What really convinced me about the deal were the conversations with the previous management team. When we discussed the field partner's new ideas, the managers were supportive and revealed that they hadn't had the capacity or the energy to pursue these strategies, although they thought the strategies were good. It seemed to me that this acquisition would create value right off the bat because of the new management and its next steps.

The toughest thing in making these investment choices is committing to a decision. You have to commit and then go. I sometimes feel that if I hesitate midway, it's like sitting in the intersection, and I realize that I'm less safe than I would be if I made a choice and committed to it. At the same time, I always like to know that if things go wrong, I have an exit strategy of my own. I always *design my business divorce while all the parties are still in love.* The goal in any investment, of course, is to have a long-term, prosperous relationship. But, given that, you never want to be stuck in a losing situation. In Wealth Cycle Investing, there is no room for getting stuck. That's why you should always include a getting-unstuck plan—a business divorce—in any investment deal papers.

> *Design your business divorce while all the parties are still in love.*

There are so many assets to consider in direct asset allocation, and we are only skimming the surface when we look at real estate and private equity. I'm going to devote the next chapter to one of my favorite assets, something that the wealthy have loved for years.

11

Energy

Getting Down and Dirty with Oil and Gas

I don't own oil and gas stocks. I own the oil wells themselves. If nothing else, it's very impressive to talk about owning oil wells. Of course, there's more than prestige going on in this asset class. The history of the oil and gas industry is a terrific example of the concept of direct asset allocation and how the wealthy realized that direct participation in creating and building assets was the path to riches—even before they themselves achieved real wealth.

Before I get into that, I have to emphasize that when you talk about risk/reward in asset allocation, there are many people who will say that energy is among the riskiest investment categories. In fact, most of the prospectuses for oil and gas opportunities begin with "Oil & Gas investments are speculative in nature, and are investments involving a high degree of risk. Persons considering these investments generally must be accredited, sophisticated, and qualified to make them."

In other words, oil and gas investments almost personify traditional risk. But there are ways to take investments that are thought to be risky and make them less so. You can do this by educating yourself about the opportunity and getting a team. When I decided to get into oil and gas, I scouted the industry to learn about the opportunities. I studied the companies involved, talked to current investors, read the trade magazines, and devoured any data that I could get my hands on. What I found was fairly obvious: if the oil wells hit, you can make it big, with cash-flow returns that are staggering. But if the oil wells don't hit, you lose it all. I set my mind to finding a way to hedge the winning and the losing so that I'd win more often than I'd lose. I knew that someone must have figured out a way to do that, and I was going to find that someone.

My conversations led me to a small company in Texas that had been digging wells since the early 1970s. This family-owned business had created a revenue model that allowed investors to spread out their investment over several wells. Oil and gas is a numbers game; the more wells you dig, the better your chances of success. By aggregating the funds of many investors, the company was able to dig many wells, and it gave each investor a partial share in each well. Additionally, because the wells produce over a range of time, this simultaneous drilling created faster results and enhanced the blended return.

This strategy gave several investors the chance to share in the successful digs. Given that the angle was large numbers, the company needed a lot of investment to make it work. And it found those investors because it thought from the investors' perspective. It didn't expect the investors to take an out-and-out gamble. It made the objective to create a diversification strategy that would stem losses and sustain reward.

When my field partner, the son of the founder of the company, went into his family's business in the late 1990s, he asked two simple questions. He wanted to know how many wells a person would have to buy into in order to not lose money. The answer he got was 20. Then he wanted to know how many wells it would take to be responsible if he was investing his grandmother's last dollar. The answer he got was 100 to 150 wells. That's become the large numbers diversification model that my field partner has built and in which I participate.

I like this much better than buying oil and gas stocks because I'm bypassing the huge amounts of dollars that go into marketing and distribution and cutting right to the chase. I also like playing oil and gas this way because of the idea that it's actually a way to buy into one of the biggest drivers of the capitalist society, à la the Napoleon Hill model, and I believe it's helpful to our country's progress to promote energy initiatives that come from our own soil.

The early history of oil and gas reads like a Wealth Cycle Investing primer. Edwin Drake discovered oil in Titusville, Pennsylvania, in 1859. He was looking for a source for lighting lamps other than whale blubber. Drake took the oil that had bubbled to the surface of his hometown to the local university, where they told him that this substance could create a lot of resource material, including kerosene. The invention and commercial introduction of the internal combustion engine created a huge demand for gasoline, another by-product of oil. Soon there were investment groups and management teams and drillers and distributors. These were similar in organization to the Wealth Cycle teams. There was a leader, a field partner, the management and laborers, and lots and lots of OPM. People all over Pennsylvania, West Virginia, Ohio, and Indiana were getting in on this new game. Soon this new industry was off and running, built with the help of these wealth-building, entrepreneurial teams.

Big oil production in the United States got going in Texas in 1910 when Pattillo Higgins drilled down to the then-unfathomable level of 3,000 feet beneath a huge layer of shale (and doing this was also unfathomable) and found barrels of trapped oil. Higgins and his Spindletop oil field investors later created Gulf Oil and Gas Company and began the real push of oil and gas production in the world. By 1945, 90 percent of the world's oil was coming from a 45- by 10-mile area in Texas called the Black Giant. After World War II, Winston Churchill said that had it not been for American oil, the Allies would not have won the war. In 1948, Standard Oil discovered some shallow huge-producing wells in Saudi Arabia, and the Middle East came into the game.

There is still a huge amount of oil in the United States. In fact, we are the only country in the world with a natural gas highway system, and 50,000 wells are drilled in the United States every year. Yet there is the perception in the United States that we must get our oil from other countries rather than domestically. Investing in oil and gas exploration right here in the United States can be, and has been for me, an incredibly profitable and worthwhile business venture. One of the problems with producing oil is that discovering it and getting it delivered is expensive and can take a while. In the United States, that means drilling down 25,000 feet into 400-degree heat at pressures of 10,000 pounds per square inch. That's a hostile environment for sure. As we all know, most companies measure performance on a quarterly basis, and the markets tend to reward public companies for this short-term performance. Look at what's happened to research and development in any field in the last few years and you see the funds for long-term initiatives dwindling when the market doesn't value the money placed in potential.

Fortunately, for those of us who are involved in direct asset allocation, none of that matters. As I said, I don't own the stocks; I own shares in the actual wells, and I'm on an oil and gas team that is both well organized and richly diversified, so that I have the opportunity to make strong returns while managing my risk. There are only a dozen major oil and gas companies in the world because it's tough to get organized and stay alive in this business. But companies like the family-owned oil and gas company with which I've partnered have decided to build their business much like Edwin Drake.

This model of being directly involved in oil by investing in the producers goes way back; even Exxon and Conoco started this way. Today, we're doing the same thing. This is one of the investments I am most passionate about because I believe that my direct participation is helping to build something important. This company is now a $50 million investment, and I'm enjoying cash-flow returns that would shock you.

Don't think the big financiers haven't come knocking on my field partner's door. I asked him why he's working so hard to build this company and share the wealth when he could just take the money and run. He says that too many of the owners of small oil companies took the 20 to 30 P/E and became billionaires overnight. They forgot the greater cause of generating energy for our country. He's decided that being a paper billionaire isn't his vision. His vision is similar to mine: to shut off our dependency on foreign oil, build an energy company for the people by the people, and have thousands of Americans reap the profits of their own consumption. My field partner is building a company for the little guys, like Dee Newton, to get in on.

Direct ownership of oil and gas is not, no pun intended, a liquid investment. There's no real exit strategy or appreciation; the reward is cash flow. It takes some buildup, maybe six to nine months to get the well online, but then, there it is: cold, hard, crude cash. Usually, I get the equivalent of my principal back in about three years, and then it's all profit from there on (see Figure 11–1). In the meantime, I get intangible drilling cost deductions (an industry word for depreciation, although it goes against ordinary income, not passive income) as soon as the drills start spinning. If we don't hit oil, we can write off 100 percent of our investment in year one. If we hit oil, we get to write off 75 percent of our investment in year one. Of course, I then have to pay tax on the cash flow as ordinary income, but I can also continue to reinvest that cash in oil and gas and watch my profits compound. There's also another bonus called a *depletion allowance*, which means that 15 percent of production income in oil and gas is tax free. This was created by the government in order to create incentives for production in the United States. That's right, 15 percent of oil and gas profits are not taxed.

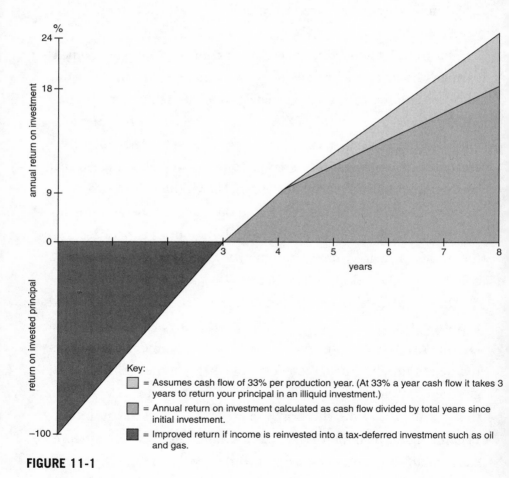

Key:
☐ = Assumes cash flow of 33% per production year. (At 33% a year cash flow it takes 3 years to return your principal in an illiquid investment.)
☐ = Annual return on investment calculated as cash flow divided by total years since initial investment.
■ = Improved return if income is reinvested into a tax-deferred investment such as oil and gas.

FIGURE 11-1

I like assets that are capital intensive (anything that requires investment in heavy equipment counts) because these assets, equipment, or property are depreciated. Let me further clarify depreciation. Although they call it "intangible drilling cost deductions" in oil and gas, other capital-intensive industries call it "depreciation," so we'll use that term here. Each industry handles depreciation differently. In accounting, however, if you buy a piece of equipment for $10,000, you do not write off that whole amount at the time you make the purchase. Businesses match expenses to the revenues those expenses generate when they generate them. If the life of that equipment is, for instance, 40 years, you should write off the cost of the equipment over that 40-year life. That means that for each year you're generating revenue, you're also writing off an expense against it. If this is done using what's called straight-line depreciation (the same amount is written off each year), then in this case there would be $10,000/40 or $250 per year of equipment expense.

Most likely, though, the $10,000 went out the door the year the piece of equipment was purchased. But while that may be the true path of that cash, it is not the accounting path of the cash. Of course, that's the reason why accounting profits and losses are different from the real cash coming into and going out of the company. This accounting rule, depreciation (in the case of soft goods, it's called "amortization"), is helpful for minimizing taxable earnings each year. As a result, assets that allow you to depreciate or amortize expenses against your revenues are always a welcome part of any asset allocation.

Traditionally, the intangible drilling cost deduction was one of the appeals of oil and gas for the wealthy. They were willing to take the risk of loss because they could use the depreciation, or a loss, against other income. As nice as the depreciation might be, most of us aren't looking for that type of tax strategy. We want assets that have depreciation without losses.

A Better Plan

Currently, only a few inner-circle individuals enjoy the real wealth that investments in oil and gas create. Anyone else who wants in has to settle for distant and marginal participation through shares in publicly traded oil and gas corporations. With some modification of the average mindset, the average investor might become interested in owning oil wells. We could literally spread the wealth by getting people to direct their money to companies like the one in which I'm invested. These are companies that have well-managed oil-producing assets that aggregate capital, organize and diversify investments, and systemize a large-scale network of thousands of investors, each of whom benefits from the profits and tax strategies of participating in oil and gas.

Getting In on Oil and Gas

Let's look at how our cash-poor millionaire, Dee Newton, might have looked at this investment. As I mentioned in her Gap Analysis, Dee took $100,000 of the $300,000 in assets she was restructuring and put it into oil and gas. She was looking at 50 wells. Given the probability that any given well will hit, she projected that these might create 3 percent cash flow a month after the 18-month ramp-up.

Dee's Money Rules guided her toward cash-flow-generating assets, and although her net worth goals were interesting, they were not that helpful at the time. Cash flow was the problem for Dee now.

However, understanding the oil and gas asset class would take self-educating.

As we've noted, with a million in net worth, Dee was in fact an accredited investor. Her worksheet looked like this:

DEE NEWTON'S	
WEALTH CYCLE INVESTING WORKSHEET	

ASSET UNDER CONSIDERATION:
Oil and gas

CONTACT PERSON(S):
One of Loral's field partners

—SETUP—

SOURCE OF FUNDS:

Wealth Account	OPM	OPI	Bank	Loan	**Restructuring of Other Asset**

Dee used $300,000 of her $1,220,000 from home equity (refinanced at 8 percent), mutual funds, and IRAs for direct asset allocation. $100,000 of this would go into oil and gas.

ENTITIES:
Dee decided to put this investment in an LLC that held a private equity investment that she'd made.

FORECASTING:
Dee deducted related expenses, including her portion of the intangible drilling cost deductions and initial losses.

—MONEY RULES—

ROI GOAL AND PROJECTED
Dee's eventual goal of $30,000 a month cash flow on $3,000,000 of invested assets would require just 12 percent ROI. But in order to get to the $3,000,000 in invested assets, Dee needed higher-than-average annual ROIs on her investments, and here she was shooting for 30 percent or more.

CASH FLOW	**APPRECIATION**
100%	*0%*
ACTIVE	**PASSIVE**
	Though passive, Dee would have the opportunity to talk directly to management, visit the wells, and make ongoing decisions about her investments.
	(continued)

DIVERSIFICATION

| Allocation | Risk/Reward | Exit Strategy |

ALLOCATION: Dee was now in real estate, promissory notes, and private equity, and this was another aggressive move for her. She still had a lot of her assets tied up in the underperforming assets that she had when she started, but for now, Dee was comfortable with this balance.

RISK/REWARD: On many levels, including cash creation and energy concerns, Dee liked the idea of oil and gas. But she understood that it was at the high end of the risk/reward spectrum.

EXIT STRATEGY: There's no liquid market for oil wells. The goal is not appreciation and sale of the well, but rather to make the money back, and then some, in cash flow.

—TEAM—

LEADER: Dee Newton

FIELD PARTNER: Loral's oil and gas field partner

MENTORS: A friend of a friend who knew the oil and gas industry

PROFESSIONALS: Lawyer, entity specialist, bookkeeper

UTILITY PLAYERS: Dee hired a part-time assistant to help her organize her house and her life. She also got a housekeeper one day a week, because millionaires get their life supported.

—DUE DILIGENCE—

DATA	DISCUSSION	DISCOVERY	DIAGNOSIS	DECISION
Internet	Field partner	Internet video tour	Strength: Opportunity for huge returns	Yes
Company's material	Industry experts	Trip to view asset		
			Weakness: Chance that no wells will produce	

Oil and gas is a big game, and it's not for the faint of heart. But if you can put a team together and get your sequencing right, you will improve your chance of success and minimize your risk.

12

Alternative Assets and More

Passion, Purpose, and Profits

In building your Wealth Cycle, you will need to be scoping out new investment prospects constantly. Everything will start to look like an opportunity, and life will become one big due diligence adventure. It's important that you always stay aware of your Money Rules, but be open to new opportunities. Many of my best investment ideas have come from colleagues or clients. It's not just financial thinking that helps you to find good investments; a good deal of creativity is necessary as well.

After all, someone had to conceive of every single financial and business concept in the first place and there's no reason that the next great investment idea can't be yours.

> *Always stay aware of your Money Rules, but be open to new opportunities.*

Let's look at some more asset allocation opportunities.

Public Equity and Debt

Some of you will want to keep a portion of your money in stocks and bonds. I've seen too many people jump into the markets to get in on the latest trend. And too many times they get into the latest fad just before the fall. Do your due diligence and use your team to help in your evaluation. Invest in companies that you believe in, ones that you believe to be good long-term investments.

When you are considering stocks and bonds, you need to do the same due diligence and risk assessment that you would with other assets. It's important that the particular industry in which your company competes fits in with your diversification strategy and that the stock or bond meets your cash flow and appreciation criteria.

Stocks can provide both cash flow and appreciation. Some stocks distribute their earnings to their shareholders through dividend payments, and some retain their earn-

Stocks can provide both cash flow and appreciation.

ings for growth. Both types of stocks can appreciate, although those that pay dividends tend to, although they don't always, appreciate at a slower rate. There are great stocks out there that pay healthy dividends and offer appreciation. Investors can look to buy the stocks that best fit their Money Rules.

There are several types of bonds. There are bonds issued by the federal government, and many of you may have one or two of these tucked away from a gift you received as a child. These U.S. Treasury bonds come in different shapes and sizes, but most of them have a low interest rate. The risk is usually nil. Then there are municipal bonds, which are the bonds issued by states and cities. These usually carry a higher interest rate than U.S. Treasuries, because they carry more risk. The risk is that the local government will go bankrupt. This is not a big risk, but it can happen. The most popular municipal bonds are tax free, which makes the return all the greater. Another type of bond is a corporate bond. Corporate bonds are the debt issued by companies through public markets. Corporate bonds usually have a higher interest rate than Treasury or municipal bonds because they carry more risk, i.e., a company is more likely to default than a government. There are also corporate bonds with very high interest rates, sometimes called subdebt or junk bonds. As you may have already guessed, these provide higher rewards because they have higher risk. Junk bonds are usually issued by companies that do not have the best credit rating.

Bonds provide cash flow in the form of interest payments, and that's why they're called fixed-income securities. They can also appreciate. Bonds trade on the open markets. When interest rates change, bonds become more or less valuable, depending on how their interest rate compares to the going rate. For example, if you have a bond that pays 12 percent a year and the going rate is 4 percent, the price of your bond is going to be a lot higher than what you lent the company. Bonds that can be converted into equity also provide appreciation opportunities.

As you get closer to your ultimate Freedom Day goals, you're going to have less need for higher-than-average ROIs, and you may want only to maintain the wealth you've built. A few specific stocks and bonds may be easier to manage than your current assets and might fit your needs, both lifestyle and investment, better.

Private Debt—Promissory Notes

Just as there's a way to do private equity instead of public equity, there are ways to do private debt. This is done by selling debt as an asset in order to collect interest. I'm a fan of selling debt as an asset.

Collecting interest at a fixed rate is as good as any cash-flow-creating hard asset.

Collecting interest at a fixed rate is as good as any cash-flow creating hard asset.

If you don't have a network within which you can comfortably sell your debt and collect reliable interest, there are other places you can look in order to become your own banker. There is currently a huge business in what's called hard money lenders. These are professionals who borrow money from individuals like you at 12 to 14 percent, then turn around and lend that money to real estate value buyers who renovate and flip, charging a point more than they are paying. These are asset-based lenders who don't really care about the borrower's credit or history, because they have the asset as collateral and/or they believe the buyer is getting the house cheap enough to make the deal profitable. The hard money lenders, by the way, are not doing just this one deal with your money. They try to flip that money three or four times a year, so they grab almost 5 percent off your contribution. But meanwhile, you're still making a nice 12 to 14 percent. Search the Internet for any local real estate clubs or organizations where people are paying cash for houses and you'll find the names of the hard money lenders. Be sure to do your due diligence on your hard money lenders.

Though we are dealing with debt, which was higher on the balance sheet than equity and thus supposedly has lower risk, keep in mind there is still risk. There's always risk in any investment. The term "defaulting on a loan" doesn't come out of nowhere. In leading your wealth, it's your responsibility to ensure the reliability of your borrower, to get the legal contracts in place, and to set up provisions and plans for the default.

Real Estate

Due diligence is taxing and time consuming, and it's hard to muster the energy to do this if you're not that interested in the investment. Investing is personal, and as you attempt to diversify your portfolio, you may find that there are only so many asset classes that you like. If that's the case, then it's important that you keep adapting your thinking and creativity within that asset class.

Jed Stone was aggressive about getting into other classes, but he found that he really liked real estate and wanted to do more of it. Through one of his mentors, he found a development company in New Hampshire that was focused on residential properties, mostly duplexes and single-family homes. He also then found a high-end development lot in an upscale division of half-million-dollar homes outside of Boston. Eventually, Jed became involved in preconstruction deals in Georgia, flipped houses in western Massachusetts, and was part of a condominium deal in Washington, D.C.

Truly Self-Directed IRAs

Most people I work with have large portions of their net worth in various retirement accounts, including pension plans, 401(k) plans, and the many different types of IRAs. We have been led to believe that we can hold only investments like stocks, bonds, and mutual funds in these types of accounts. You can now unlock and direct certain retirement accounts yourself. Self-directed IRAs allow you to invest directly in different types of real estate such as single-family investment properties, duplexes, commercial buildings, ministorage warehouses, mobile homes, and land acquisitions, to name just a few. Also little known is the fact that you can use certain IRAs to invest directly in mortgages, promissory notes, tax lien certificates, factoring programs, real estate options, business opportunities, and much more. The rules for using your IRAs and retirement accounts do require some familiarity on your part, and it pays to study up and start taking control of your retirement assets. You can get more information on ways to self-direct your IRAs and retirement plans at IRA@LiveOutLoud.com.

I have many colleagues who get very involved in one area. One field partner is into mini-storage. Another colleague likes junkyards, and yet another is investing in auto parts stores. One group of investors is buying little mom-and-pop janitorial supply and cleaning companies in small towns in the Midwest. Their objective is to acquire up to a dozen companies and create efficiencies, such as streamlining management, building online communications systems, and aggregating supply and materials purchasing. This strategy of buying small businesses and creating these synergies is often called a roll-up.

It also provides a good example of how asset addiction can have a snowball effect. The team leader noticed that in several of these markets there was no affordable housing for the company's employees. Many of them had to commute several miles to the janitorial jobs in office parks. He talked to the chamber of commerce in each of these towns about the problem of housing lower-wage workers. In most cases, the chamber of commerce members knew that the town needed affordable housing, but they weren't in favor of mobile home parks or other similar ideas that previously had been presented to them. The group got together with some local real estate developers to purchase raw land. It's now working with one of these cities to create affordable housing. The government has agreed to put in the sewers, the water, and the gas and create tax incentives if this team builds the streets and houses.

Investment and business synergies of this type can also be created within your team. If you know that a colleague of yours is buying a commercial property in town and another colleague is buying up some small airplanes to dock at the local airport, you might want to contribute to this burgeoning boomtown with a limousine service to take those executives back and forth. This kind of building and development thinking is how the fabric of this country was created, and those who continue to build its networks and organizations will benefit from its growth. The excitement about the architecture and connectivity of the Internet and the World Wide Web is the same type of pioneer thinking. Unfortunately, those pioneers got too far in front of the intrinsic value they were creating. I believe that the investors who continue to, and those who begin to, apply that frontier thinking to the original playing fields, like land, and even expand to other out-of-the-box areas, like natural resources, will enjoy the growth and wealth that those ideas will generate.

> *Look to create investment and business synergies within your team.*

This idea of one venture leading to another fits with what I previously said was the crown jewel in Napoleon Hill's treatise. This team of Millionaire Makers became part of what Hill called that "unseen power." They were not just investing in capitalism; they were becoming capitalists themselves. By buying into, and helping to create, the world in which we live, they were now the people who "organized that power." I find that very exciting.

Those Intangible Intangibles

Buying into any asset is hard enough, but buying into an asset that relies heavily on intangibles is even harder. Of course, most investment opportunities originated as the seeds of someone's imagination and creative thinking. It is how close your investment is to that beginning and how much the conceptual part of the operation still plays a part in its success that becomes the issue at hand. Most ongoing businesses or products that are on the market are far from the original idea, yet some of them still rely heavily on the concept portion of the asset—that is, the idea still matters. This is usually true in exciting and glamorous investment sectors, such as leisure and entertainment. Here we're talking about hotels, restaurants, sports franchises, and movies, to name a few.

I recently began investing in a restaurant created by one of my field partners. He'd been in many different businesses and industries and had seen assets from many sides. Despite the perception that restaurants are risky, he believed that if you focus on your due diligence, all investments come down to the same fundamental checklist.

This is the type of investment that belongs to visionaries. Real estate developers take empty space and make it into a home, an office, or sometimes a landmark building. Movie makers, software developers, and inventors take an idea and make it into a global happening. Though investing in an idea can be very risky, it can also be very rewarding.

And that's one of many reasons that I invested in this restaurant: because the risk can be managed, and restaurants can be very rewarding. I know that some people invest in these assets because they want to be able to say, "I own a restaurant." And I'm sure I've done that at a party or two. Fundamentally, though, when I did my due diligence on this opportunity, I was looking at my checklist: the concept offering, the management, the market, the industry and the competition, and the numbers.

From concept to numbers, my due diligence checked out. But I needed a few more facts to pull me in. I was curious as to why restaurants had such a bad rap as investments, and I needed more information. There were several things that I found out during my research. First of all, food is a trillion-dollar-plus industry, and it's one of the largest segments of our gross national product. The rumors are true: people are eating. Second, my colleague showed me projections that soon over half of all meals, literally 53 percent, were going to be "out of home," which means restaurants, food courts, fast food, take-out, and delivery. Obviously, there are businesses that provide these out-of-home meals, and some of them would be rewarded for their efforts. But the restaurant sector was highly competitive and relied heavily on concept.

The concept is the secret ingredient in the leisure and entertainment industries. This is the intangible asset that can create success for one company and disaster for another. As much as I bought into the fundamental checklist, the fickleness of foodies made me realize that I had to believe in the intangibles. My field partner believed in his idea. He had an energy and passion for food and was excited by the pure game of entrepreneurship. Of course, that pretty well characterizes most entrepreneurs.

Basically, it came down to my gut. After looking at the fundamentals and considering the intangibles, I decided to get into this restaurant. And it worked out for me and others on our team. I bought into the first restaurant, and a second is on the way.

There's no way you can be sure about any investment. They all have risk. But in your asset allocation sometimes it's worth it to consider some of these high-risk, high-reward assets that rely on intangible assets like concept. At the very least, they are exciting and fun.

Nickels and Dimes: The Big Business in Small Businesses

Frank W. Woolworth built his millions on nickels and dimes, and you can too. Though some would beg to differ, cash- and coin-generating businesses, like car washes, video arcades, casinos, and Laundromats, are about as far from the glamorous intangibles I just mentioned as you can get. Although, with a few clever marketing schemes thrown in, they are getting a bit more glamorous these days. You might have noticed that these businesses, as well as various trade routes for vending machines, are for sale all the time in local business broker newspapers. Some of these are better than others, and knowing what to look for and the right questions to ask is vital to success. Vending routes, for example, can be a big hassle to service and maintain, and some routes have poor foot traffic or poor security. Car washes obviously need to be in busy areas, where the land is usually expensive. Video arcades have to maintain the current technology, and Laundromats have to compete with the downward pricing of home machines.

In looking at these cash-generating retail operations, you want to find a good ongoing concern that still has room for improvement. The factors you're looking for include market demand; a lack of competition; controlled, if inefficient, operations; and an obvious sequence that has created, or can create, cash flow. The objective is to acquire the business at a fair price, perhaps even a value price, so that you can create opportunities for future growth. The last thing you want to do is pay a premium for an asset that's going to ultimately stay flat.

Allison Connor wanted to dip her toe into small change, specifically Laundromats. She found a millionaire in the town near hers who was heavily into this asset all over Florida. She asked him to mentor her.

Allison's main concerns were how to find the assets, the time and energy it would take her to manage these assets, and the when and how of her exit strategy. She began by driving around to dozens of Laundromats in and outside of Miami. She approached each owner directly, had an easy conversation, and left behind a letter stating her intention to acquire a Laundromat. After a month of this, one of the owners finally called. Allison and her mentor set up a meeting. The mentor approved of the location, the machines, and the price point. He also liked the fact that the place had video games and vending machines, and plenty of parking. The nearest competitor was 13 blocks away. They also noted that the owner was older, was moving to Phoenix, and did not want to manage the business from afar. Thus his reason for selling did not feel like leaving a sinking ship.

And so Allison moved to the next step of intent with the seller. She arranged for disclosure agreements and got the bank statements so that she could see exactly what was going in and going out. It crossed her mind to ask for a one-year lease with an option to buy so that she could experience the numbers herself. But the owner had other buyers interested in immediate acquisition.

Following much due diligence, including lots of information from her mentor, Allison learned that in that area, sellers tended to overprice these particular businesses. Though she had looked at the books and the numbers, she still wasn't sure if these were real. The problem with the numbers in a cash business is that sometimes the owners do not always include everything in their statements to the Internal Revenue Service (IRS). The IRS, of course, was not born yesterday, and so it has ways and means of dealing with this fact. It's not uncommon, for instance, for the IRS to make certain adjustments on its own, such as figuring out the real carry-out cash business from a restaurant based on how many so-called doggie bags the restaurant has to buy, not the revenue numbers that the owner gives it. A buyer of these assets can do the same thing during due diligence. Allison looked at the utility bills. She decided that if she checked the water usage and did a water-per-load assessment, a measurement she obtained from the water company, she could get a better idea of the real number of loads, and hence revenue.

With the help of her mentor, Allison was able to use experience and judgment when evaluating the numbers presented to her. She supplemented this advice with information from the Coin Laundromat Association, a trade group that gave her the financial equations to diagnose a healthy deal. Allison also set up an LLC so that she could use it for her revenues and expenditures and retain more of the income without dancing around numbers with the IRS. This would also help her with her exit strategy in that the next buyer would see the real numbers going in and out.

Allison found that this acquisition fit well with her skill set. She was good at problem solving, communication, and management. She felt that she could use these skills to get higher returns on her asset. Specifically, she planned to improve and emphasize the relaxing atmosphere.

Different Paths to Wealth

There's a lot to be said about different assets, and there are thousands of interesting investment opportunities. You will be amazed at the range of direct investing opportunities that you will uncover along the way. This is part of the fun of putting it all together.

The Wealth Cycle requires that those assets and opportunities meet your criteria and goals to make you a millionaire. I know millionaires who are focused on real estate, I know others whose investments consist mainly of private equity ventures, and I know many others who are in a variety of assets and asset classes and industries and ideas. No two millionaires have done it the same way. What I have found to be consistent is that most millionaires are not sitting around waiting for the next great thing to come to them. Millionaires are active and productive people. Instead of working at jobs with a fixed wage and an ultimate salary cap, the wealthy have been, and are, out there creating businesses and pursuing entrepreneurial ventures, and using that money to invest in and develop more assets. That's the secret prescription to building wealth that the wealthy understand. And now you do too.

13

Putting It Together

Compounding Power

The Wealth Cycle is very much an integrated approach that begins with your Financial Baseline. This is followed by a vision of your Freedom Day, which then leads to a Gap Analysis. You can then get your Cash Machine and your assets (the Wealth Cycle Investing pieces) in motion, supported by entities, forecasting, Wealth Accounts, and debt management. And throughout the process you will need to fully engage your foundations of leadership, teamwork, and conditioning.

These are the 12 building blocks of the Wealth Cycle. Though you will use each building block throughout the wealth-building process, the most important thing is to sequence these blocks properly, that is, to do the right thing at the right time, so that you can achieve optimal results.

How Jed Stone Got from Nothing to Something

Let's revisit one of our investors and see how, specifically, the Wealth Cycle accelerated his wealth. Starting with nothing, Jed is an interesting example of how to sequence the building blocks in the Wealth Cycle. We started by

1. Establishing Jed's Financial Baseline
2. Establishing his Freedom Day
3. Conducting his Gap Analysis

    The next step in Jed's sequence, was the

4. Cash Machine

    Jed set up an

5. Entity

    to manage this and to

6. Forecast

    his revenues and expenditures through that entity. He began to live a corporate life. Once the business was up and running, he made steady payments from the Cash Machine into his

7. Wealth Account

    And while his Wealth Account grew, Jed also

8. Managed his debt

    Jed then started looking into

9. Assets

Jed scoped out sectors and industries, collected information, and began to contact possible mentors, all of which helped him build

10. Leadership
11. Conditioning
12. Teamwork

These were skills that he knew he'd need to lead his wealth. That was Jed's Wealth Cycle sequence.

The Millionaire Maker Plan

In four months, Jed had formed the habit of making a Wealth Account priority payment. He had set up an LLC for his gym resale business, and in that LLC we set up a holding account, that is, a corporate Wealth Account. He then lent that money to another LLC that was specifically designed for investing in new assets. The Cash Machine then had a promissory note in its assets column, a loan made to the investing LLC. Though this is aggressive, I think it is worthwhile for wealth builders to take at least 10 percent of the earnings generated from their Cash Machine business and allocate this money directly to invest in other assets. When Jed eventually took this Cash Machine business online, he began generating several thousand dollars a month. With the money building up in his Wealth Account, Jed made his investments.

The First Real Estate Deal

We kept this simple. Jed, along with a friend, bought a little cash-flow-generating house in bread-and-butter America. He paid $3,000 and realized $100 a month cash flow. Eventually, Jed bought more of these houses.

The Second Real Estate Deal

Now that he'd seen how to do these deals, Jed wanted to try it on his own. He went to a market in upstate New York, found a field partner and a team, created an LLC, collected OPM from mentors and friends in Boston, and purchased 15 cash-flow-generating homes. He put no money into the deals and, after a 50–50 split with his field partner, collected $300 per house in up-front fees and received $10 a month per house in cash flow. Eventually, Jed bought more of these homes and was able to increase his participation in both equity and cash flow.

Private Equity

Being comfortable with OPM and eager to accelerate his Wealth Cycle, Jed conducted due diligence on various private businesses. He then invested $10,000 in one of his mentor's colleagues' private manufacturing companies. This provided 20 percent annual cash flow for his revenue stream and had the potential for appreciation. Private equity was of great interest to Jed, and he continued to invest in other companies and ventures.

Oil and Gas

Jed was now ready for the big guns. He found OPM and put $10,000 into oil and gas wells. After 18 months ramp-up, during which he enjoyed the intangible drilling cost deduction benefit of this asset, Jed was getting a 3 percent per month cash return on his investment.

And On and On . . .

Jed became a true asset addict. He wanted to buy more and more. This tends to happen when the money's rolling in. That's why the wealthy are usually the most careful with their money. It's difficult to get someone to spend $1 when they know how much they can make on that $1 if they invest it. Though Jed continued to enjoy his lifestyle, he was no longer living beyond his means, and his expenditures remained flat.

We diversified Jed's asset allocation toward the lower-risk, lower-reward buckets with some steady growth, blue chip stocks he picked, as well as promissory notes.

Promissory Notes

Jed favored these in his asset allocation. He eventually had several thousands of dollars of these in his portfolio, each paying an average of 12 percent annually for a period of anywhere from three months to a year.

More Real Estate

As I mentioned in the previous chapter, Jed really got going in real estate. He got into New Hampshire duplexes and single-family homes, high-end development lots near Boston, preconstruction deals in Georgia, flips in western Massachusetts, and condos in

Washington, D.C. Jed accumulated a lot of cash through the flips. In flips, you're looking for the operating efficiencies I mentioned in the due diligence section on discovery. In this case, Jed went to flat markets and looked for properties that were situated in prime locations in terms of demand, but that had seen better days. Jed put in a little money and some muscle and fixed them up. The prime location part was important. You can fix up a house all you want, but if it becomes that tree that falls in the forest and no one hears it, then you've got just another pretty house, tired muscles, and less cash. I helped Jed to structure these deals for almost all OPM or debt, in a pattern similar to that of the leveraged buyouts favored for the acquisition of various companies. Jed was getting very much into a pattern of using no cash down to create cash flow, and he'd entered the big leagues.

With these investments, Jed realized another secret that the wealthy have always understood: a mortgage is a mortgage is a mortgage. The paperwork and wrangling required for a $100,000 deal are the same as those required for a $40,000 deal. And that's what the wealthy and Wall Street bankers, and anyone else who does deal after deal, has always known: that doing a big deal is just as hard as doing a little deal, so you might as well do the big deal.

Jed gave a few land deals a look, too. He found areas that he thought would appreciate, using easy landmarks for these growth trends, such as the building of a large chain store, the development of schools, or zoning for an airport.

In or Out

At this point, Jed got involved with the janitorial supply and cleaning company roll-up. And this led to the affordable housing development. Jed stayed out of assets that involved intangible assets and creative concepts. He found the due diligence difficult to execute and the data frustrating to grasp. Although I was in some of the deals that he rejected and vice versa, I respected Jed's approach. He was taking responsibility, being accountable, showing initiative, and being resourceful. Jed practiced future pacing when drawing up his revenue models, filled his team with bigger, better brains, and found colleagues who could do the work so that he didn't have to. He was truly leading his wealth.

More and More

This is when Jed realized that things were getting exciting. He was getting wealthy, and he was investing like the wealthy, stretching upward on the risk/reward scale. He now had a viable organization of entities overseeing multiple streams of revenue, made up of his fully functioning Cash Machine and a diverse range of assets in which he was directly involved, including real estate, private equity, and oil and gas.

Jed collected more OPM, invested in properties and businesses with several different field partners across the country, and realized annual returns of 20 to 30 percent on his investors' investments. Most of this was in cold, hard cash flow that went right into his, and his investors', hands.

Returns of 20, 30, 40, or 50 percent and higher are very possible for anyone in Wealth Cycle Investing. This requires learning about the specific asset in which you're interested, gathering a good team that has knowledge of this asset, and, very importantly, creating some action, by which I mean deals. You have to take action in order to get the experience you need to gain confidence and get these results. You will not start with these high-level returns. I've seen many who get into real estate realize only a 4 to 6 percent return on their first deal. But the education is worth the price, and if you learn from your mistakes, you can eventually make your way up that risk/reward scale.

Team

In addition to getting better at using OPM and creating cash flow, Jed was reminded time and again how important the team is. I'm convinced that without a team, even the best asset performers are hindered. My field partners tend to be very smart, energetic, straightforward, and focused on nothing but their business. I've had a few field partners who suggested that they might want to try their hand in a few of my other businesses. I invest in and believe in people, so I always gave this a fair shot. This worked when the field partner expanded his or her reach to become involved in additional classes within the asset that he or she already knew. It failed when a bright field partner stretched into fields that were unrelated to the assets that she or he had worked so hard to understand. Diversifying your assets is a great idea, but your brain and your body only have so much capacity. I like learning a lot about a lot of things, but as the captain of my ship, I want the sailor who's pulling up the sails not to worry about keeping the deck clear. Playing one's position and playing it well makes teamwork work.

Jed was excited. He felt that he was moving along well in a short period of time, which fit in with his low patience and high energy level. He now realized, by doing it and not thinking about it, that the idea of generating and accelerating wealth through a Wealth Cycle was viable. What I think shocked him a bit was the momentum that was inherently built into this process. With Jed's foundation firmly in place, his targets clear, and the sequence of the building blocks in his Millionaire Maker plan arranged almost effortlessly in a right time, right place zone, Jed's wealth building accelerated even more—through better financing.

Financing His Deals

Once Jed had established a track record, he decided to look at the possibility of using bank debt for some of his deals. The benefit here is a lower cost of funds and a larger share of the equity on the upside. Giving away equity to get partners is, if the company is successful, an expensive source of funds, or, as those on Wall Street say, a high cost of capital. If you're able to pay a low fixed interest rate on a loan, you can enjoy a much larger portion of the upside. The downside of debt, of course, is that if the deal is not successful, you need a way to pay it back. That's why most banks want to see a track record of success before they give loans. And since Jed had that track record, he was a good candidate.

I introduced Jed to the idea of going to the little local banks where he could build personal relationships. Most of these banks want to help their communities prosper, and they may take a special interest in helping you.

Another way to finance deals is through the owner of the asset itself. Jed's experience had also made him better at negotiating deals. When he was looking at a small distribution business, I suggested that he raise the idea of owner financing with the seller. The owner wanted one big payment up front, and when Jed asked if he could make the payment over five years, the owner almost laughed him out the door. But we were prepared for that. We'd asked a tax attorney on our team to draw up the tax benefits of taking the money over five years. When we showed the owner that he'd actually be getting more money this way, he stopped laughing and signed the papers.

Joint venturing for equity is an excellent way to accelerate and finance your Wealth Cycle Investing. To learn more about how to use OPM and about the details of deal structures, e-mail retours@liveoutloud.com.

"Old Jed's a Millionaire"

After this, everything rolled. Jed accelerated his investments in every bucket of his asset allocation. As he became known as an investor, Jed discovered that finding ventures that needed money wasn't difficult, but finding the right ones was. Deal after deal seemed to land at Jed's door. He got very picky about due diligence, and got the help of a lawyer, an accountant, and a financial analyst to find the select few that he would consider. He continued to invest in a variety of industries and sectors, always thrilled with the prospects. As you saw, the assets in which Jed was invested included promissory notes; some specifically chosen public stocks; both cash-flow-generating and appreciating real estate, ranging from land deals and preconstruction to commercial real estate; private equity in business ventures, from new product development to retail chains; and oil and gas. Jed had come a long way from the guy who had nothing.

Your Portfolio

Your direct asset portfolio, once you are fully engaged in the Wealth Cycle Process, will look far different than what you have now. Most people have their money in their home, 401(k)s, and IRAs, and, through these, they are invested in stocks, bonds, CDs, and so on— indirect assets with middlemen taking a piece of their money. Here are a few examples from our wealth-building community of how they set up direct investing portfolios:

Direct Asset Investments					Indirect
Real Estate	Private Equity/ Businesses	Notes	Cash/Liquid	Gas and Oil	Stock Market
30%	30%	10%	10%	10%	10%
40%	30%	10%	10%	10%	
50%	30%		5%	15%	

You will learn over time what works for you and the returns you are after. Personally, I like all direct investment assets and balance them with market trends, strategy and team. You too can be an "asset addict" when you get commited to taking control and leading your team and your wealth.

Jed's is but one story; your plan could well look different, but the building blocks are always the same in Wealth Cycle Investing. Wealth building is a dynamic and continuous process, and you, with the right sequencing, team, and knowledge, will achieve your Freedom Day far sooner than you can possibly imagine.

And then, the best thing that we can all do is pass our learning and experience along to the next generation.

14

The Next Generation

Building Baby Millionaires

Children, grandchildren, nieces, nephews, friends' kids, students . . . Guess what? These little people don't need your money. What they need is your knowledge. This generation will benefit most from your wealth building if you teach them how to model what the wealthy do, by giving them a chance to model you. If they learn how to live in a Wealth Cycle, they can make their own money and generate their own assets. And they can start earlier than you think.

My son, Logan, has been involved in my Millionaire Maker Plan since he was a toddler. Now he's seven, and he asks who's going to live in the houses we buy and how much they're going to pay us every month. He wants to know what's going on with the oil wells we own, how many have hit, and if we can actually get the oil out. He suggests certain companies that might be interesting to look into, especially if they make cool toys. His latest interest is the Laundromat we purchased; he visits it weekly to get the coins out of the machines and help count the money. And it goes beyond the conversation. Logan works for my company, Live Out Loud, doing odd jobs, modeling, and helping out at the seminars. We pay him a little salary, and that's his current Cash Machine. He puts a priority payment into his Wealth Account and some into his Roth IRA, and when he sees an asset that he thinks might be a good investment, we talk about it, do our due diligence, and decide if we should follow through or not.

It's amazing to me how easily these concepts come to kids. They don't have all those barriers that you and I grew up with. Logan knows that assets can create more assets, which means more money for him. This makes him eager to invest now and wait to buy the bike, knowing that he can get a better bike by first building his wealth.

There are several exercises you can do with your children to get them on the road to asset addiction. Begin with their own Big Table. Suggest that they get together with friends, cousins, or neighbors and talk about money. You can ask them questions about money and steer them toward the benefits of wealth, including being able to help others through charitable donations and creating good businesses. You might also suggest that they put a portion of their allowance into a Wealth Account. Additionally, setting up an entrepreneurial venture in order to get more money than their allowance is a fun activity, and it gets most kids excited because it's doing something real. It will probably take them a while to generate much money, but you can help them begin the asset allocation portion by letting them join you in your

Seat your kids at the Big Table.

investments. If they have a share of your real estate deal, they can receive part of the cash disbursements, as well as enjoy the appreciation on the assets. Nothing teaches better than doing, and this is a great activity that you can do together.

This is not the piggy bank model. This is the only expansive model out there. We are growing, not stowing away and slowing down. It's important to teach this at an early age, to instill in children better ideas than we had. Childhood is about hope, not fear, and your children will probably take to the aggressive, go-for-it model that we're building here. Everything in this book is just common sense, and if we'd all learned it early on, it wouldn't be scary at all. Share this education with your children. It will mean more to them than any check you could ever write. Remember, this is different, not difficult. You, and they, can do it.

Final Words

I'm not sure if it's a choice or a genetic disposition, but it seems to me that there are two ways to go through life in this world: with optimism and with fear. I believe that if people believe in themselves and in others, they can achieve wonderful things. In fact, I'm pretty sure that all the wonderful things in this world came from those who achieved through faith, not fear. There are those who will read this book and say, "I fear this is impossible; there's too much to lose." And there are those who will say, "I believe this is possible; there's so much to gain." I promise you, it's possible; I'm proof of it.

The Wealth Cycle will not work for you if you are a perfectionist, if you're afraid to make a mistake, and, most importantly, if you're afraid to fail. I've made a lot of mistakes, and I've had a lot of failures, and I do not know any successful wealth builder who can't say the same thing. In order to succeed, you have to fail. There's just no two ways about it: you must fail your way to success. Those who succeed right off the bat usually do so with too much madness and not enough method, and we all know that those who get what they want quickly usually lose it just as quickly. Wealth building is a slow and steady process, but it is not a small process. It takes big courage and faith in yourself and others.

I've come a long way from waking up too early to walk the beans on a farm in Nebraska. My work is now very rewarding; I have an educational business that helps thousands of people every day, and I have a Wealth Cycle that will sustain my family and me for generations. I accomplished this because I know that if people believe in themselves and in others, they can achieve wonderful things. You can do this, you can be a millionaire. You just have to take action and believe.

Index

A

A money, 28

Accelerating returns, 25

Accessible assets, due diligence for, 99–102

Accredited investors, 11–12

Acronyms, 80

Action, as basis of Wealth Cycle, 13, 24–25, 45

Active investors, 46, 63–64

Adaptability, 67

Amortization, 175

Analyses:

    comparable, 124–125

    numbers in, 118–122

Analyses (*Cont.*):

    ratios in, 122–123

    valuation, 116–118

Appreciating assets, 46

    bonds as, 181

    private equity ventures as, 158

    real estate as, 139

Appreciation:

    cash flow vs., 58

    in Money Rules, 61–63

Assessing assets, 25–27, 88–94

Asset Accelerator software, 27

Asset addiction, 184

Assets, 7–18
  and accredited investor status,
    11–12
  appreciating, 46
  assessing, 25–27, 88–94
  attitudes needed for increasing,
    15–16
  to avoid, 125
  on balance sheet, 110–111
  building, 6
  cash-flow, 46
  of Cash-Poor Millionaires, 39, 41
  current, 122–123
  direct allocation of (*see* Direct
    asset allocation)
  guidelines for developing, 16
  intangible, 93
  millionaire-making, 3–4
  new opportunities for, 179
  real estate as entry into, 140–150
  relying on intangibles, 185–187
  researching, 21
  restructuring, 29
  for Restructuring Assets
    investors, 39
  team of mentors for investing
    in, 12–13
  types of, 17
  for unaccredited investors,
    13–15
  valuation of (*see* Valuation)

Assets (*Cont.*):
  in Wealth Cycle, 19
  (*See also specific types of assets*)
Awareness, 67

B

B money, 28, 29
Balance sheet, 107, 110–113
Biased information, 81
Big Table, 206
Bonds, 180–181
Book value, 123
Brand equity, 89
Breakeven analysis, 117
BusinessWeek, 21

C

C money, 28, 29
Capital, 18
Capital Development, 115
Capitalism, 17–18, 185
Car washes, 188
Cash flow, 120
  appreciation vs., 58
  assets for, 46
  from bonds, 181
  in Money Rules, 61–63
  from private equity ventures,
    158

Cash Machine, 13–14, 37

Cash-flow statements, 107, 113–116

Cash-generating businesses, 188–190

Cash-Poor Millionaire (Type 4) investors, 2

assets for, 8

Gap Analysis for, 39–55

oil and gas investment for, 176–178

Casinos, 188

Checklists, 86–88

Children, Millionaire Make Plans for, 205–207

Churchill, Winston, 172

Coin-generating businesses, 188–190

Colleagues, on team, 74

Commitment to creating wealth, 5

Comparable analysis, 124–125

Comparables, 91

Competition, information on, 91

Conditioning, 15

Conoco, 173

Consciousness, financial, 33

Continuous investing, 19

Contracts, 74

Corporate bonds, 181

Courses of study, 82

Creativity, in finding investments, 179

Current assets, 122–123

Current liabilities, 123

Current ratio, 122

Current situation, Money Rules and, 57–58

D

Data collection:

in due diligence, 79–83

for manufacturing and distribution company, 99–100

for real estate, 95–96

Deals, finding, 22–23

Debt, 112

on balance sheet, 111

good vs. bad, 148

private, 181–182

public, 180–181

Decision:

in due diligence, 94

in real estate investing, 98

Depletion allowance, 174

Depreciation:

deductions for, 54–55

on income-producing real estate, 145

for oil and gas investments, 175

Diagnosis:
  in due diligence, 94
  for manufacturing and
    distribution company, 101
  for real estate, 98
Direct asset allocation, 6, 9–10
  for accredited investors, 12
  individual control in, 16
  responsibility for, 78
Direct assets:
  due diligence for, 99–102
  languages of investing for, 80
Direct participation programs
    (DPP), 6, 9–10
Discounted cash-flow analysis, 117
Discounts, 121
Discovery:
  in due diligence, 86–94
  for manufacturing and
    distribution company, 101
  for real estate, 97
Discussion:
  in due diligence, 83–86
  for manufacturing and
    distribution company,
    100–101
  for real estate, 96–97
Diversification:
  within an asset class, 65
  to balance portfolios, 46–47
  in direct asset allocation, 9

Diversification (*Cont.*):
  of information sources, 82
  Money Rules for, 29–30, 64–68
  in private equity ventures, 159
  in real estate, 150
Dividend yield, 123
Dividends, 120
DPP (*see* Direct participation
    programs)
Drake, Edwin, 171
Due diligence, 23–24, 77–102
  art of, 77–79
  data collection in, 79–83
  decision in, 94
  diagnosis in, 94
  for direct and accessible assets,
    99–102
  discovery in, 86–94
  discussion in, 83–86
  on hard money lenders, 182
  as leadership requirement, 74–75
  levels of, 78
  for manufacturing and
    distribution company, 99–102
  for public equity and debt, 180
  for real estate, 95–98, 183
  for Something from Nothing
    investors, 35
  sources of information for, 79–80
  on Wealth Cycle Investing
    Worksheet, 30

E

Earnings, 120

Earnings-to-equity- ratio, 123

EBIT, 115–116

EBITD, 116

EBITDA, 116, 121

Economic risk, 131–132

Energy investments (*see* Oil and gas investments)

Entities, business (*see* Structuring entities)

Entrepreneurship, 5

Environmental risk, 93, 132–133

Equity, 112–113
   on balance sheet, 111
   public, 180–181
   (*See also* Private equity ventures)

Exit strategy, 47, 167

Experience:
   to find hidden numbers, 124–125
   learning curve with, 69

Exxon, 173

F

Fear, 209

Field partners, 22–23, 71–72

Financial Baseline, 20
   cash flow in, 58
   in Gap Analysis, 31

Financial consciousness, 33

Financial Freedom Day, 20

Financial objectives, 57–58

Financial statements, 107–116

Financials, of potential investments, 93–94

Financing risks, 134–135

Fixed-income securities, 181

Flexibility, 66–67

For Sale By Owner (FSBO), 150–151

Foreclosures, 151

Fortune, 21

401(k) plans, as source of funds, 43

$400 solution, 73

Freedom Day:
   in Gap Analysis, 31
   goals for, 46

FSBO (For Sale By Owner), 150–151

Future pacing, 154

G

Gap Analysis, 31–55
   for Cash-Poor Millionaire investors, 39–55
   due diligence in, 51–53
   entities in, 44–45
   IRAs in, 43–44
   loans in, 42

Gap Analysis (*Cont.*):

    Money Rules in, 45–47

    refinancing in, 42

    for Restructuring Assets
        investors, 37–39

    for Saving to Delay Spending
        investors, 36–37

    for Something from Nothing
        investors, 32–36

    team in, 47–51

Gas investments (*see* Oil and gas
    investments)

Goal return on investment, 59–61

Goals, financial, 20, 57–58

Goodwill, of potential investments,
    93

Gross profit, 119

Growth investors, 61–63

Gulf Oil and Gas Company, 172

H

Hard money lenders, 182

Hidden numbers, 123–124

Higgins, Pattilo, 171–172

High-risk, high-reward investing,
    4, 12

Hill, Napoleon, 17–18, 185

History of industries, 91

Holding accounts, 68

House, as traditional investment, 3

I

Income assets, real estate as, 139

Income investors, 61–63

Income statement, 107–110

Increasing sales, 119

Industry, understanding, 91

Industry risk, 132

Information:

    absorbing, 81–82

    evaluating, 87

    finding, 79–81

    for risk reduction, 4

    sources of, 82, 85

    (*See also* Due diligence)

Intangible assets, 93

Intangibles, assets relying on,
    185–187

Intellectual property, of potential
    investments, 93

Investing:

    continuous, 19

    high-risk, high-reward, 4, 12

    learning about, 21

    optimizing choices in, 68

    responsibility for, 23–24

    traditional, 3

Investments:

    assessing, 25–27

    ideas for, 17

    passive, 16

    potential of, 104

Investors:
    accredited, 11–12
    active, 46, 63–64
    growth, 61–63
    income, 61–63
    passive, 46, 63–64
    types of, 1–2, 7–8
    unaccredited, 13–15
    value, 62–63
Investor's Business Daily, 21
IRAs, 183–185
    investing funds from, 28
    Roth, 43
    self-directed, 44, 183–185
    as source of funds, 43–44
    as traditional investments, 3

J
Jargon, 80
Junk bonds, 181

K
Knowledge:
    needed for real estate, 155
    for risk minimization, 10

L
Land, 151
Languages of investing, 80

Laundromats, 188–190
Leader, team, 70–71
Leadership rules, 74–75
Leading questions, 84
Learning about assets, 21
Lectures, 82
Legal issues, for potential
    investments, 93
Leverage, 28–29, 60
Liabilities:
    on balance sheet, 111
    current, 123
    of potential investments, 93
Lifestyle, earning, 33–34
Limited liability companies
    (LLCs), 24
Liquidation of investments, as
    source of funds, 29
Liquidity, 110–111
Liquidity ratio, 122
Live Out Loud Web site, 45
Living out loud, 15
LLCs (limited liability companies),
    24
Loans, as source of funds, 42

M
Management:
    of potential investments, 92
    of risk, 127, 137–138

Management risks, 136

Manufacturing and distribution company, due diligence for, 99–102

Margins, 109–110, 119

Market share, 119

Marketing information, 90

Marketing plan, 37

Mentors, 6, 21–22
   for Saving to Delay Spending investors, 37
   in selection of field partners, 23
   for Something from Nothing investors, 35
   on team, 72–73
   team of (*see* Team)

Millionaire(s):
   commitment to becoming, 5
   self-made, 30

Millionaire Maker Plan:
   example of, 195–203
   in Gap Analysis, 31
   for next generation, 205–207
   for Something from Nothing investors, 34
   team defined by, 34

Millionaire-making assets, 3–4

Mini-warehouses, 152

MLS (*see* Multiple Listing Service)

Modeling risks, 135–136

Money:
   classifications of, 27–28
   sources of, 28–29
   on Wealth Cycle Investing Worksheet, 27–29
   working hard for, 4–5

Money Rules, 57–68
   for active or passive investments, 63–64
   in building assets, 20
   for cash flow and/or appreciation, 61–63
   and current situation/objectives, 57–58
   defined, 29
   for diversification, 64–68
   in Gap Analysis, 45–47
   for goal and projected ROI, 59–61
   purpose of, 57
   in Wealth Cycle Investing, 68
   on Wealth Cycle Investing Worksheet, 29–30

Multiple Listing Service (MLS), 150, 151

Multitenant buildings, 152

Municipal bonds, 180–181

Mutual funds, as traditional investments, 3

N

Net present value (NPV), 117
Net worth, 58
New investors:
    in oil and gas, 176–178
    private equity ventures for,
        164–167
Next generation, Millionaire Make
    Plans for, 205–207
No-limit thinking, 58
NPV (net present value), 117
Numbers:
    becoming familiar with, 106
    hidden, 123–124
    in valuation, 118–122

O

Oil and gas investments, 169–178
    for Cash-Poor Millionaire
        investors, 176–178
    diversification in, 65
    getting started in, 176–178
    history of, 171–172
    in oil wells vs. stocks, 169–175
    risks with, 170
    tax deductions for, 174–176
Oil wells, 4, 169–175
Operating profits, 119
Operations, information on, 90–91

Operations risks, 135
OPM (*see* Other people's
    money)
Opportunities:
    information on, 88–89
Optimism, 209
Options, real estate, 152–154
Organization, of potential
    investments, 92
Other people's money (OPM):
    for real estate, 140
    for Something from Nothing
        investors, 35
Ownership structure, 106 (*See also*
    Structuring entities)

P

Paperwork, 42, 44
"Park and pray" model, 9
Partners, on team, 74
Passive investments, 16, 140
Passive investors, 46, 63–64
Pay-yourself-first concept, 20
P/E (price/earnings) multiple,
    120–122
Pensions, as traditional
    investments, 3
Perceived risk, 15, 77
Perishable spending, 33

P&L (profit and loss) statement, 107

Plan, for direct asset allocation, 10

Portfolio:

building, 5

diversifying, 46–47, 67

guidelines for developing, 16–17

million-dollar, 3–4

Potential of investments, 104

PPM (private placement memorandum), 99–100

Preforeclosures listings, 151

Price/earnings (P/E) multiple, 120–122

Primary home, as traditional investments, 3

Private debt, 181–182

Private equity ventures, 4, 157–167

advantages of, 158–159

for new investors, 164–167

objectivity in, 162–164

personal interest in, 159–162

Private placement memorandum (PPM), 99–100

Privately placed investment opportunities, 14–15

Pro forma financial statements, 108

Product risk, 130–131

Professionals, on team, 73

Profit and loss (P&L) statement, 107

Profitability ratios, 123

Profits:

gross, 119

operating, 119

Projected return on investment, 59–61

Promissory notes, 181–182

Public equity and debt, 180–181

Q

Quantitative value, 107–116

Questions:

asking, 83–84

in asset assessment, 88–94

by multiple persons, 88

unasked, 130

R

Ratios, 122–123

Real estate, 4, 139–155, 183

depreciation deductions for, 54–55

diversification within, 65, 150

due diligence for, 95–98, 183

as entry into assets, 140–150

future pacing with, 154

Real estate (*Cont.*):
  hard money lenders for, 182
  higher-than-market-average
    returns on, 14
  land, 151
  mobile home park example,
    130–136
  multitenant buildings, 152
  options on, 152–154
  residential, 150–151
  in self-directed IRAs,
    183–184
  slowness in build-up of, 149
  for Something from Nothing
    investors, 140–148
  specific knowledge needed for,
    155
Real estate investment trusts
  (REITs), 21
Real estate options, 152–154
Real risk, 15, 77
Refinancing, as source of funds, 42
Reinvesting profits, 25
REITs (real estate investment
  trusts), 21
Researching assets:
  due diligence in, 23–24
  for general investing knowledge,
    21
Residential real estate, 150–151

Responsibility:
  for investing, 23–24, 70
  for risk, 87
Restaurants, 186–187
Restructuring Assets (Type 3)
  investors, 2
  assets for, 8
  equity ventures for, 164–167
  Gap Analysis for, 37–39
Retail businesses, 188
Retirement plans, self-directed, 184
Return on equity (ROE), 123
Return on investment (ROI):
  accelerating, 25
  for accredited investors, 11
  calculation of, 33
  compounding, 81
  creating more assets with, 19
  goal vs. projected, 46, 59–61
  higher-than-market-average, 14
  for income strategy vs. growth
    strategy, 61–63
  speculative, 61
  use of term, 81
  in valuation, 122
  in Wealth Cycle Investing, 6
Reverse timelines, 163–164
Risk(s), 129–138
  with bonds, 180–181
  economic, 131–132

Risk(s) (*Cont.*):

    environmental, 93, 132–133

    as failure to educate yourself, 4

    financing, 134–135

    in high-reward ventures, 4

    industry, 132

    management of, 127, 137–138

    management risks, 136

    minimization of, 10

    modeling, 135–136

    with oil and gas investments, 170

    operations, 135

    with private debt, 182

    product, 130–131

    real vs. perceived, 15, 77

    reducing, 42, 69, 136–138

    responsibility for, 87

    strategy, 135–136

    valuation, 134

    in Wealth Cycle Investing, 6, 68

Risk factors, 134

ROE (return on equity), 123

ROI (*see* Return on investment)

Roll-ups, 184

Roth IRAs, 43

S

Sales, 119–120

    increasing, 119

    information on, 90

Saving to Delay Spending (Type 2) investors, 2

    assets for, 7

    Gap Analysis for, 36–37

    small business investments for, 188–190

Securities and Exchange Commission (SEC), 11, 14

Self-directed IRAs, 44, 183–185

Self-made millionaires, 30

Selling properties, 154

Sequencing, 163, 164

Setup, on Wealth Cycle Investing Worksheet, 27–29

Small businesses:

    as investments, 188–190

    rolling up, 184

Something from Nothing (Type 1) investors, 1–2

    assets for, 7

    Gap Analysis for, 32–36

    real estate for, 140–148

    Wealth Cycle example for, 194–203

Source(s) of funds, 28

    on cash-flow statements, 113

    for Cash-Poor Millionaires, 41

    IRAs as, 43–44

    loans as, 42

    refinancing as, 42

Spending, perishable, 33

Standard Oil, 172

Start-up companies, 4

Stocks, 170–175, 180

Strategy risks, 135–136

Structuring entities, 14, 24

   for Cash-Poor Millionaires, 41

   in Gap Analysis, 44–45

   for Restructuring Assets
      investors, 39

   for Saving to Delay Spending
      investors, 37

   on Wealth Cycle Investing
      Worksheet, 27–29

Subdebt bonds, 181

Success, 209–210

Supply and demand relationships,
   92

Synergies, 184–185

T

Target market information,
   89–90

Tax issues:

   with bonds, 181

   deductions for oil and gas
      investments, 174–176

   depreciation deductions, 54–55

   depreciation on income-
      producing real estate, 145

   and diversification, 66

Tax issues (*Cont.*):

   for income vs. growth
      investments, 63

   for potential investments, 93

Team, 69–75

   for diversification decisions, 67

   field partners on, 71–72

   in Gap Analysis, 47–51

   gathering, 12–13

   leader of, 70–71

   leadership rules for, 74–75

   mentors on, 72–73

   partners and colleagues on, 74

   professionals on, 73

   purpose of, 69

   for risk minimization, 10

   rules for, 74–75

   for Something from Nothing
      investors, 34

   utility players on, 73

   on Wealth Cycle Investing
      Worksheet, 30

Team Made Millionaire seminars,
   82

Tenant-buyers, 154

Think and Grow Rich (Napoleon
   Hill), 17–18

Timelines, reverse, 163–164

Traditional investing, 3

Trends, industry, 91

Trust, LLC ownership by, 24

Type 1 investors (*see* Something from Nothing investors)

Type 2 investors (*see* Saving to Delay Spending investors)

Type 3 investors (*see* Restructuring Assets investors)

Type 4 investors (*see* Cash-Poor Millionaire investors)

U

Unaccredited investor, changing status as, 13–15

Unasked questions, 130

"Unseen power," 185

U.S. Treasury Bonds, 180, 181

Utility players, on team, 73

V

Valuation, 103–127

  analyses in, 116–118

  comparable analysis in, 124–125

  from financial statements, 107–116

  help with, 126

  hidden numbers in, 123–124

  methods of, 125–126

  numbers in, 118–122

  objective factors in, 104–105

Valuation (*Cont.*):

  ratios in, 122–123

  risk factors in, 127

  subjective factors in, 104

Valuation risks, 134

Value investors, 62–63

Vending machines, 188

Video arcades, 188

Vision, 58

W

Wall Street Journal, 21

Warehouse buildings, 152

Wealth:

  different paths to, 190–191

  secret of, 18

Wealth Accounts, 20

  for children, 206

  dual, for personal and LLC use, 54

  investing funds from, 28

  portion of returns into, 25

Wealth Cycle, 2–3

  action in, 24–25

  building blocks of, 5–6, 193

  criteria and goals in, 190–191

  no-limit thinking in, 58

  for Something from Nothing investor, 194–203

Wealth Cycle Investing, 1, 19–30
    assessment of assets in, 25–27
    due diligence in, 30
    interconnection of building
      blocks in, 68
    Money Rules in, 29–30
    objective of, 6
    personal responsibility in,
      23–24
    setup of money and structures
      in, 27–29
    steps in, 20–25
    strategies for, 5
    team in, 30

Wealth Cycle Investing Worksheet,
    25–27
    due diligence on, 30
    Money Rules on, 29–30, 59
    ROI numbers on, 60–61
    setup on, 27–29
    team on, 30, 70
Weekend-in-the-streets tours, 82
Woolworth, Frank W., 188
Workshops, 82

Y
Yields, diversifying, 65–66, 120

About the Author

LORAL LANGEMEIER is the author of the national bestseller *The Millionaire Maker,* a master coach, financial strategist, and team-made millionaire who reaches thousands of individuals each year. She is the founder of Live Out Loud, a coaching and seminar company that teaches her trademarked program Wealth Cycles.